Who's Walking Around in Your Head with Muddy Boots?

New Tools for Self-Discovery and Self-Healing

Sabra J. House, LCSW

Illustrated by Patti DuBois

Bloomington, IN   Milton Keynes, UK

AuthorHouse™
1663 Liberty Drive, Suite 200
Bloomington, IN 47403
www.authorhouse.com
Phone: 1-800-839-8640

AuthorHouse™ UK Ltd.
500 Avebury Boulevard
Central Milton Keynes, MK9 2BE
www.authorhouse.co.uk
Phone: 08001974150

© *2006 Sabra J. House, LCSW. All rights reserved.*

No part of this book may be reproduced, stored in a retrieval system, or transmitted by any means without the written permission of the author.

First published by AuthorHouse 4/18/2006

ISBN: 1-4259-1660-0 (sc)

Printed in the United States of America
Bloomington, Indiana

This book is printed on acid-free paper.

Acknowledgments

To Lou Evers for becoming editor, photographer, project manager and the primary reason that this book is now being published. She gave me the confidence and courage to approach this book once again because she saw it as valuable and worth the time and effort it would take to have it published. She also wanted to ensure that this dream of mine came true.

To Dr. Ashley Conner who read the manuscript with love and then encouraged her mother to be brave and optimistic about publishing it.

To Todd House who reacted to what I wrote and thought everyone should write a book about his or her life experiences.

To Irene Conlan for always seeing me as someone who could have a book published.

To Ron Pike who read the book with love and the eyes of a critic.

To Julie Ohlinger for suggesting that I write this book in the first place.

To Emily and Ethan for sharing their creativity, their unfiltered wisdom and their spiritual gifts.

To Patti DuBois for volunteering her time and her incredible talents. Her ideas and her drawings brought the book to life and me too, as an author.

To my patients who provided the wonderfully creative answers and the windows to their souls.

To the Universe for providing me with this new and challenging lesson, over and over again!

Thank you one and all!

Contents

Introduction ix

Chapter 1: What Animal Would You Like To Be? 1
    Discover your personal values and priorities

Chapter 2: How Tall Is Your Wall? 17
    Learn about your trust level and your defenses
    Discover your perception of love and support in your life

Chapter 3: Who's Walking Around In Your Head With Muddy
    Boots? 37
    Identify the negative thoughts that live in your head
    Discover tools for dealing with these thoughts

Chapter 4: What Color Is Your Aura? 55
    What you think about is visible
    Become aware of auras and discover ways to see them

Chapter 5: How Clean Are Your Windows? 73
    Discover decisions made in childhood
    Learn to use affirmations for change and growth

Chapter 6: What's Your Scarecrow Doing Now? 85
    Discover ways to identify and solve personal
      problems through imagery

Chapter 7: What Does Your Path Look Like? 103
    Your current path provides a sense of purpose and direction
    See how it differs from your spiritual path
    Learn to use affirmations for assurance

Conclusion 119

Introduction

This is a book about discovering tools for understanding yourself. It is directed toward people who want to grow and change. It is designed for those who want deeper insights into themselves and who wish to develop creative ways of dealing with the challenges in their lives. It is for those who have some sense that they are on a purposeful path and are not quite sure what that path is all about. This book will lead you on a treasure hunt and you will come to discover that the treasure and the answers are within you.

The writers and therapists of today talk about using affirmations, visualizations and meditation. These are wonderful methods and have worked well for me, but many people are not familiar with them or have not been able to use them effectively. This book talks about tools you can use to discover who you are, what you think and what is true for you. These are simple tools that anyone can use. These tools uncover knowledge and information that come from inside you, rather than from outside of you.

The tools described in this book come in the form of questions – projective questions I began asking myself and my patients many years ago. They are simple questions that lead to answers that can be interpreted, explained and understood. The ultimate goal is for these answers to lead to self-knowledge, personal growth and enlightenment. Wayne Dyer says, "The door to enlightenment opens inward." I think that this book, <u>Who's Walking Around In Your Head With Muddy Boots?</u> will help you open that door.

Many authors, like Louise Hay and Laura Davis have written books and then later wrote workbooks for them. My book is both a book and workbook. I am affectionately calling it a "working book." It is geared toward people interested in psychology, self-help, personal growth and spiritual development. It is directed toward an audience who seeks answers from personal growth seminars. It is for therapists and for people in therapy. It is for people who want to explore their inner-selves with or without the assistance of a therapist. It is a means to self-discovery, self-maintenance, and self-healing.

Who Am I?

I'm a psychotherapist with a Master's Degree who has helped people heal and grow for twenty-five years. Ten of those years were spent working as a therapist in a clinic in Michigan. Then I was drawn to Arizona and began writing this book while waiting for my private practice to grow. The book contains many examples drawn from my first ten years as a psychotherapist. It contains other people's answers to the questions of "Who am I?" and "What am I all about?" It contains interpretations of these answers as well, so that the reader has the benefit of experiencing the questions first and then learning what others have said in their responses. Finally, in addition to my professional interpretations, I have provided the reader with powerful tools; each opens the inner windows of awareness and understanding.

And so I share with you my "Crazy Questions," which have led to growth for myself as a therapist and marked improvement for my patients. Your responses to these questions are subjective. Your interpretations will have to come from inside you and they will have to be based on intuition, insight and sensitivity. There are few guidebooks in this area and there are no absolutes.

The first chapter asks the question, "If you could be any animal in the whole wide world, what animal would you like to be?" and "Why?" There are working pages available for answers to these questions followed by examples drawn from my years of practice. The result is that readers can begin to draw conclusions about their own answers and can begin to understand themselves.

The second chapter talks about walls. We all have a wall between us and our world. How tall is your wall? How thick is it? What's it made of? What color is it? When you look down, what are you standing on? And when you look up, what do you see? The answers to these questions can provide valuable information about anger, hurts, ability to trust, emotional support and future orientation. Examples from other patients help provide opportunities for comparison and understanding.

The third chapter is about identifying and controlling negative thoughts. I had a Loch Ness Monster who used to raise her ugly head and make disparaging remarks about everything I tried to do. By identifying her and doing battle with her I learned a lot about the damaging effects of negative thoughts and how to stop this process. The question asked in this chapter is "Who is walking around in your head with muddy boots?"

The fourth chapter is about seeing auras. I discovered, during the years of doing therapy, that sometimes I could see colors about the head and shoulders of my patients. I'd use this information to give them a gift of information, from themselves — to themselves. I also learned to ask patients, young and old, if they could see colors. A lot of them could. One patient was not aware that there was anything to be seen until the moment I talked about the existence of auras and then she said, "Oh, you mean that orange color around you?"

I think auras are important, because auras do not lie. They reflect us just as we are. To be able to see auras around others is a gift that can be reclaimed. To become aware of our own aura and what we're sending out can make us more responsible for our thoughts and feelings. Reading this chapter can plant seeds of awareness in those who didn't know auras existed and can challenge others to work at perfecting this gift. It's an exciting opportunity. The title of this chapter is "What Color Is Your Aura?"

The fifth chapter is about the lens through which people view their worlds. I've discovered during my years of doing therapy that people make decisions in childhood that influence the rest of their lives. The decisions are unconscious and remain below a conscious level of awareness, but continue to impact adult lives though beliefs about love, trust and worthiness. This chapter gives readers the opportunity to discover their own negative childhood decisions and to learn how to counteract those decisions through the use of affirmations. Affirmations need to be specifically tailored to counter the negative childhood decisions. Unfortunately, if affirmations are too positive, they will be rejected. So this chapter discusses the best ways in which affirmations can be used without creating internal resistance.

The next chapter talks about asking for answers in the form of symbols. It's about going within and asking for a picture or a symbol to define the problem. The reader has something concrete to work with and something to monitor change, as there is personal development and growth. One of the examples provided in this chapter is a woman who, when she asked for a sign or symbol, got a scarecrow. It was a perfect symbol for what she was experiencing in her life. She could see herself as this scarecrow and could mark her own progress as the symbol evolved and the activity around it changed. I titled the chapter, "What's Your Scarecrow Doing Now?"

The last working chapter is about paths. "What Does Your Path Look Like?" I believe we're all on a path; it's just that many people aren't aware of that fact. If you could be made more aware, perhaps you would put more effort into personal growth and less effort into worrying about how to get where you are going. I've had readers draw their paths, meditate on their paths, or use the method described in the previous chapter to discover what their paths look like. This chapter offers the reader the opportunity to do the same. Having the sense that you are on a path can relieve some of the anxiety related to living. Awareness of this path can assist you, the reader, in seeing life experiences as lessons to learn from, rather than punishment or merely random purposeless events. "Path awareness" can provide a much needed sense of purpose and direction.

Windows are all about openings and letting in light. It is my hope that through the "windows" provided by this book, you can look into yourself and begin to discover who you really are and what you really feel. Hopefully, it is through windows such as these that you will discover the treasures within you and the treasure that *is* you!

Sabra J. House, LCSW

Chapter 1:
What Animal Would You Like To Be?

What Animal Would You Like To Be?

Here is your first opportunity to learn something about yourself. You get to ask yourself two questions about animals. The best answer is the first thing that comes into your mind. Even if this answer seems silly or stupid, write it down. If the answer that comes to you is not even an animal, but a member of some other family, write it down. There are no wrong answers.

First, ask yourself **"If I could be any animal in the whole wide world, what animal would I like to be?"** On the workbook page provided, write down the first thing that comes into your mind. Usually there is an instantaneous flash across the brain as an idea streaks by, but, because you're so accustomed to there being a right answer and you've never been asked this question before, you're probably not very sure of your response. Don't worry if it's right or wrong. Be confident. It's ok. Sometimes when working with a patient, I've had to add that it doesn't exactly have to be an animal and it doesn't even have to exist on this planet. There are no limitations to the answers to this question!

Secondly, **write down three reasons why you've chosen that animal.**

Next, answer this, **"Of all the animals in the world, which one would I *not* want to be?"** Proceed again to write down three reasons why you don't want to be this animal (or reptile or insect or whatever it is you've chosen).

Workbook Page

1. If you could be any animal in the world, what animal would you like to be?

_____

2. Write down three reasons why you would like to be that animal.

_____

_____

_____

3. Of all the animals in the world you would not like to be, what comes to mind?

_____

4. Write down three reasons why you would not like to be this animal.

_____

_____

_____

Good - you've done well. Now let's look at some examples so you can see how other people have responded and what their responses meant.

One 50-year-old woman said she would like to be a *cat* because they're soft, independent and people like them. She wouldn't like to be a *snake* because they're slithery, not attractive and people don't like them. The *cat* and the *snake* are not nearly as important as the fact that she wants and needs to be liked by people. We then began work on her priority of having people in her life that liked her. We also worked on her sense of self-worth and her being worthy of having people like her.

Another woman also selected a *cat* because they're their own person; they stretch, move and have a free body. She wouldn't like to be a *snake* because of their reputation of sliminess, being sneaky and the assumption that they can be fatal. These are the same two choices, but the reasons are very different. This woman had had a mastectomy. See how it is reflected in her choices? There might have been a loss of choices for her. There had been a loss of body freedom. Movement is not what it once was, so she would like to be a *cat* whose movements are very free. The choice of the *snake* reveals the underlying fear that the cancer will sneak up on her once again and be fatal.

An 18-year-old girl chose a *horse* because it is big, strong, clumsy and sweet. She didn't want to be a *snake* or a *turtle* because they're on the ground, can't see anything, are slow, too small and get stepped on. The opposites here are being big and strong like a horse as opposed to being little and stepped on. This young woman had been cast out of the family when her parents divorced and neither parent really wanted her to live with them. She had lost a lot – her home, her family and her confidence. She needed to be strong in order to survive in her new world, and she needed to avoid being stepped on by others' insensitivity. The snake and turtle also represented loss of vision – her inability to foresee the divorce.

Another young girl also had opposites. She chose a *bird* – because it goes anywhere, flies and sees everything. She didn't want to be a *worm* because they can't go anywhere and have to go so slowly. Movement, autonomy and independence are strong values with teenagers and adults. We want to be strong and mobile versus insignificant, little and vulnerable.

Opposites can be expressed in terms of what we see, our range of vision or sense of freedom. One young mother said she would like to be an *owl* because they're wise and they can fly. She then thought she wanted to be a *sea gull* because they're freer than *owls*. But she didn't want to an *anteater*, because they have long tongues, they eat bugs and their nose is always stuck in the ground. The ground became the grindstone, and she felt very stuck indeed, with much to do and few choices.

A woman who lost much through a divorce and now had no one significant or loving in her life said she wanted to be a *dog* because most people like dogs, they get a lot of attention and are really cared for and loved. She didn't want to be a *snake* because people are afraid of them, don't like them and they're not very loveable. Notice the need for love and attention she mentions. According to her, the opposite is true for snakes.

A word is needed here about *snakes*. When I first began asking these questions, *snakes* appeared often in the answers and I wasn't sure just how to interpret this choice. I thought the snake represented basic evil or a sexual symbol from the unconscious. I eventually came to realize that the snake symbolizes powerlessness and helplessness because it is on the ground. The snake has no arms and no legs. For us, arms and legs symbolize our ability to make things happen, the ability to move, to be autonomous, to stand on our own two feet. The fact that snakes can make things happen and get where they wish is important only to snakes! Snakes crawl on their bellies, and that too has a negative connotation for us. We speak of crawling on our bellies when we are afraid or are seeking to please. This is not considered a noble gesture. Finally, snakes are not well liked by most people. Snakes are then chosen when people strongly value being liked.

For instance, a gentleman struggling through a middle age crisis and the mixed feelings regarding an affair said he wanted to be a *lion* because they are King of the Jungle, have sexual prowess, have sleekness, power, strength and good hair color. He didn't want to be a *snake* because they are sneaky, slithery and evil. His use of the lion represented masculinity and the command he sought over his life. The snake represented his guilt and anger about his own behavior, which went against his value system.

Another gentleman of 30 began with the same choices. He also wanted to be a *lion* because of their tremendous strength, family orientation, confidence and strong ability to survive. He didn't want to be a *Chihuahua* because they're weak, have a bad reputation and bark all the time. Notice the opposing values – strong versus weak, positive and powerful versus negative and yappy. Early in our sessions he had mentioned his concerns about his own sexuality and that explained his choice of *a lion*, one of the major symbols of virility and maleness. We began work on his sexual identification and his emotional independence.

Another gentleman, who was having difficulty with relationships, described these choices, he wanted to be a *bird* because they have a good outlook on life, there's a large variety of them and they never get fat. He didn't want to be an *animal in the zoo* because they're confined, have limited space, and a lack of freedom. Notice that all three say basically the same thing. Freedom, space, lack of confinement were important to him. This man feared confinement and fled from commitment, hence his relationship problems. When his values were identified for him during our work together, he could look at them and weigh the value of freedom versus the value of a loving, committed relationship. He could then make a decision knowing what his values were, rather than reacting to them in an unknowing fashion.

One young girl wanted to be a *zebra* because they are strong, different and unique. I found this a brilliantly creative choice for her, as she was the daughter of a racially mixed couple. Two years later she wanted to be a *great white shark* because they are pretty in their own way. Some time after that she wanted to be a *black panther* because they "look neat" and can basically do whatever they want to do. Unconsciously she portrays the struggle of her heritage. First the *zebra* who is half black/half white, then the *shark*, which she describes as a white one. Notice the increase in anger inherent within the choice. And then notice the shift to the *panther*, still an angry choice, but now powerful and very definitely black.

As we evolve, our choices change and our reasons change, too. We are not static. We are constantly reflecting what is going on around us and inside us. In a way these answers are a way of taking a reading of what is going on inside.

One woman, struggling with her value system regarding an affair, said she wanted to be a *cat* because they were cuddly, furry, sophisticated and independent. She didn't want to be a *mouse* or a *rat* because they were sneaky, small and got into things they shouldn't. Her conflict was between needing affection and doing as she liked, versus being sneaky and dishonest. When the conflict became apparent to her through her own words, she then made decisions based on awareness of her value system, rather than reacting to unconscious motivation or feeling stuck.

What the Images Really Mean

Are you aware that 80% of our decisions are based on our internal and unconscious value system? These are values we established in childhood and never looked at or questioned. Often we don't even know this value system is in operation. All we know is that when we go against our value system, we have unidentified or unexplained bad feelings.

The value conflict creates a vague feeling of discomfort or may be expressed physically as a stomachache, headache, tension or irritability. Ask a mother how she feels when pulled between a maternal value to care for a child and the value of extending herself to her partner. Ask a child how he or she feels to be pulled between two parents. A person wishing to get a divorce may value family and stability. The idea of divorce goes against this value system and so he or she may have emotional or physical discomfort without knowing or understanding why. They may also be unable to move forward due to the "value conflict," again, without knowing why. Another person may wish to divorce but has a value of being liked. Since there is a strong possibility that their spouse may not like them or their children after the divorce, there will be unexplained bad feelings and an inability to move forward with what they desire. Values are powerful and important. To know what yours are can assist you when you're feeling stuck and can help with decision making. The simple choice of picking an animal that you would like to be will assist you in developing a greater awareness of your value system.

To continue with examples, here is another set of choices: *kitten/cat* because they are soft, cuddly and easygoing; as opposed to being a *snake* because they are slimy and everybody is afraid of them. The opposites here are the qualities of being nurtured and being liked as opposed to being rejected and not liked.

In another instance, the qualities of being nurtured appeared this way. An 18-year-old girl wanted to be a *horse* because they are pretty, run really fast and they get brushed every day. She wouldn't want to be a *dog* because they are always getting "crapped on," they get put in the doghouse and they are supposed to be man's best friend, but they're not. This young woman wanted to feel important in her family, but she'd been sent away as a child and had never recovered from the rejection.

Survival can enter into the responses, especially when the person answering the question is a child and there has been fighting in the home. One ten year old said he would choose to be a *fish* because he liked to swim. He would not like to be a *deer* because they get shot and other animals prey on them. His sister said she would like to be a *cat* because they're frisky and they play a lot. She would not like to be a *deer* or *rabbit* because they get shot during hunting season and sometimes they don't survive the winter. A third young man, who has been separated from his mother due to an unsubstantiated charge of neglect, said he would not like to be a *salmon* because when they are spawning, they swim upstream and die before they ever get to return home. This last example was interpreted in court as a defense for allowing him to see his mother. As a result of this interpretation, the young man was allowed to resume visitation and thus "return home" on a regular basis.

Sometimes, at first glance, the choice of animal appears to be a negative one, but when the reasons are given, the answer makes perfect sense. A woman who valued relationships and a sense of belonging chose a *wolf*. Her reasons were that they have a pack they belong to and are loyal to, they mate for life and they are survivors. This same woman did not want to be a *lemming* for specific reasons. They self-destruct based on instinct, they seem to have no freedom of choice or options; they are small, helpless and lack protective instincts.

Survival continues to appear in a variety of ways. One 20-year-old girl would not like to be a *rat* because they get preyed on and they eat garbage. Another young woman didn't want to be an *ant* because they're always getting stepped on. One gentleman did not want to be a *spider* because they are so small, slow and get scrunched. Another lady did not want to be a *fish* because they get eaten all the time. And a young girl did not want to be a *mouse* because they didn't seem like they could survive very long.

The most extreme example of vulnerability and fear for survival appeared in the answers of a young woman who had never developed a sense of adequacy and for years had suffered with depression. She could not think of an animal she wanted to be because there was no animal that doesn't get hurt. And she really didn't want to be an *elephant* because they were more apt to be killed for their ivory.

Another young girl suffered terribly from allergies and as a result missed a great deal of school. She then developed a school phobia and felt extremely vulnerable. Her vulnerability and fears were expressed in these choices. She wanted to be a *puppy* because she could be somebody's pet and somebody could hold her and feed her and play with her. She didn't want to be a *deer* because she would get shot and a deer only lives for about a year.

Just when I thought that an answer was universal, someone would come along and disrupt that thought! A woman whose husband was an avid deer hunter said that she <u>wanted</u> to be a *deer* because they are graceful, gentle, caring and protective of their young. They also know how to survive and stay away from the hunter. She didn't want to be a *cat* because they are independent and cold, with an "I don't need anybody attitude." This woman's husband had separated from her, leaving her with two small children to care for. She valued survival skills, warmth and nurturing. She did not want to be independent and cold-hearted, ways she felt her husband had treated her. She also wanted to be protective of her children and survive the actions of her husband. Her choices fit perfectly, from her perspective!

Negative self-images also came through clearly. A 14-year-old who felt she was ugly said she did not want to be a *pig* because they are small, dumb and ugly. Her positive choice was a *dog* because they're mean and don't let themselves get pushed around. For women who are overweight *elephants* are frequently a "negative" choice because they're big, clumsy, dusty, dirty, wrinkled and there's nothing beautiful about them. Elephants represent being over-sized and obese, negative connotations in our media-rich world of thinness and glamour.

However, elephants do not always have a negative connotation. One man chose an *elephant* because they are big and gentle and concerned with relationships. They are kind to their young and are perceived as being very bright. Another person, this time a woman, chose an elephant because they are strong and gentle. Their premise was that elephants are good to you, if you are good to them. They care for their young and they can move mountains. So, an animal that is negative for one person can be positive for another. There are no absolutes.

On the more positive side, there are beautiful choices made by patients whose responses sound like poetry. One woman would like to be a *sea gull* because, as she said, "I'd love to soar around like that." Another woman wanted to be a *butterfly* because they are a new creation and are free to go wherever they wish. A woman who'd been in a car accident wanted to be a *white swan* because they're clean, graceful and can fly. She no longer walks gracefully. A sensitive and creative teenager wanted to be a *unicorn* because they're majestic, pure, and innocent and accept people just as they are. What wonderful and accepting values she has! And, she probably wishes people would accept her as non-judgmentally as well.

Now, go back and look at how you answered the questions. The information from yourself to yourself is in the answer you wrote down.

What can you discover about yourself?

Are your animals opposites in any way?

How are they different? Is there a difference in power between them?

Is there a difference in vulnerability? In size?

Is there a difference in likeability?

Look at the reasons you gave for why you chose your animals.

Look for qualities that are important to you.

Do your choices tell you anything about your values?

What values do they reflect?

Are they people/relationship values?

Are they strength and autonomy values?

What needs do you mention?

What vulnerability or losses do they reflect?

What people-relating values do you mention?

Do the answers reflect anything about what you are not getting in your life?

In what way are your answers creative?

In what way are your answers reflective of what is going on in your life?

—*Sabra J. House*—

What do you know about yourself that you didn't know before?

The next chapter is about a wall, about the barrier you have erected between you and your world. You'll have an opportunity to learn about your defenses, your level of trust, and how vulnerable you are. You'll learn what support there is in your life and how you perceive it. You'll learn about your future orientation and what is holding you back from achieving your goals.

Personal Notes

Questions:

Thoughts:

Actions:

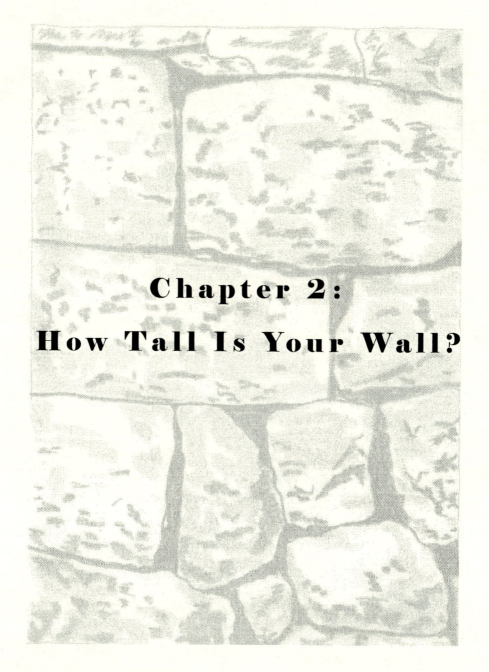

Chapter 2:
How Tall Is Your Wall?

How Tall Is Your Wall?

This question begins, "from the same place you got your *cat* and your *dog* (or whatever animal you chose,) **tell me about your wall.**" We all have a wall between us and our world. It developed from the events that happened in your life. Answer the questions about the wall even if you can't see it. Just let the answers come to the surface and write them down. There are no right and wrong answers. There are no silly answers. All answers, even seemingly illogical ones, make sense in some way.

How tall is your wall?

_____

How thick is it?

_____

What's it made of?

_____

What color is your wall?

___

Are there doors, windows or gates?

___

If so, how many openings are there and are they open, closed or locked?

___

Who might these doors, windows or gates be for?

___

If you look down, what are you standing on?

___

If you look up, what do you see?

___

Is there anything special or interesting or different about your wall?

___

When I first started using this set of questions, I thought that the patient had to see the wall to answer the questions. But somewhere along the line, I overrode that thought and told them to answer even if they couldn't see a wall in their minds (after all, not everyone is visual.) Lo and behold, the answers were there! Sometimes I asked if there was anything different or special about their wall. Occasionally there was something different or special worth mentioning and it always had meaning.

When I started, I didn't know what the answers meant. There were no instruction books on this topic. So I began to respond with intuitive interpretations, which I checked out with the patients as I went along. If my interpretation was on target they'd respond immediately. If my interpretation was off, then I'd ask what they thought it meant and usually they could come up with an answer and a meaning that fit.

The height of the wall came to represent the degree of anger present. The thickness of the wall described how much protection was needed or was missing. What the wall was made of often spoke of the hurts that had been suffered or the amount of defense that was needed. The more dense and impenetrable the material, the more often my patient had been hurt. Sometimes, though, the wall was such that it did not protect them from hurt and, as a result, they were still very vulnerable. Let me stop and give you some examples.

"It's made of bricks, a mile thick and never ending. Nobody is going to let me out," said a 10-year old in the middle of his parents' divorce.

"It's ten stories high and made of bulletproof glass. I can see out but nobody can see in," said another youngster who had been emotionally abused.

"My wall is tall; I can't get over it. It's ten feet thick and made of brick," said a young woman whose choice of lifestyle had caused her parents to disown her.

"It's red and as tall as can be. It's 3-4 inches thick and made of brick. There's one gate but it's locked," said a young teenager who'd been molested.

"My wall is paper thin, like eggshells. It's not tall enough and there is nothing on the ground," said a particularly vulnerable woman with no family support.

"It's a shower curtain that's opaque and cream colored," said a young woman who had little protection for herself and didn't want people to see who she was for fear of rejection.

"It's made of clear acrylic, but it's soundproof, and it's all around me, " said a woman who felt vulnerable and who had heard extremely bad news regarding her health. She didn't want to hear any further news on this issue, hence the soundproofing.

As I began to identify meaning for height and thickness, my next challenge was to match meaning with color for their answers to the question, "What color is your wall?" Initially, I used The Color Test written by Dr. Max Luscher and translated by Ian Scott, as a source of information. I found that his description of black fit the emotions of the patient who used it. Black, according to Dr. Luscher, "is the negation of color itself. Black represents the absolute boundary beyond which life ceases, and so expresses the idea of nothingness, of extinction. Black is the 'No' as opposed to the 'Yes' of white." Whoever chooses black for the color of their wall wants to renounce everything. They are experiencing a stubborn protest against their existing fate and feel that nothing is as it should be. Often they are in revolt against that fate, and they are liable to act unwisely in this revolt.

"My wall is black," said an adolescent whose first relationship had been an experience in being used sexually. It was a "No" to life, a major statement of "I don't care now, because somebody used me and didn't care about me." Ahead, she could see only black, meaning she felt life would never be any better. She was failing many of her classes, she was about to be dropped from the track team because of her poor grades and she said she didn't care. We looked with great seriousness at her defeatist attitude, her refusal to try and her anger at herself for being taken in. I talked about how successful she was at failing. She didn't like that approach at all. We then worked on protecting herself, being proud of herself and caring about what happened to her. Within a few weeks she had a more positive attitude, was doing well on the track team and was studying to improve her grades.

Another adolescent's wall was black and blue. Her parents had divorced some time before, and her dad had remarried. For the past three years he had picked her up one day a month, spent the day with her, but never took her to his new home or included her in his life. The black was her protest against the relationship she had with her father. She and her mother fought often. Blue can mean sadness and depression. So, from that perspective, the blue represented the relationship she had with her mother. Blue can also be identified as a desire for harmony or healing which could be her desire to resolve the issues with her mother. Actually, she was taking the angry protest about her dad out on her mother. When she could identify her anger consciously and could separate the anger toward her parents from adolescent strivings, she was better able to get a handle on her emotions. Having the angers identified and their sources noted released her from blindly "acting out."

What follows is a list of colors that frequently appeared on walls described to me. It is by no means a complete list of colors or a definitive list of meanings, but it can be used as a starting point for understanding the nuances and meaning of color.

Black	A "No" to life, a protest, hiding something, extreme frustration, "Blacking out," or blocking all possibilities.
Blue	A desire for peace and harmony, a desire for healing.
Light blue	Desire for harmony and peacefulness, lack of conflict. If there's a lack of strength in the color, it can mean immaturity.
Dark blue	Generally sadness and depression when the qualities of harmony and security are absent.
Green	Independence and autonomy, new growth.
Grey	Compromise, lack of commitment, refusal to get involved or participate. Often seen in walls of children whose parents have divorced.
Brown	A doing color, getting things done. Also, represents a lack of spontaneity or enthusiasm.
Red	Anger or rage. Generally the darker the color, the older the anger.
Orange	A doing color, with more energy and purpose than brown.

Pink	Love, but can also indicate a little girl color, or an adult who's living in a little girl world.
Peach	A combination of pink and orange, loving and doing with energy and purpose.
Mauve	A combination of red and blue, symbolizing love and harmony and energy. If it becomes purpley, there's probably a lot of fantasy or creativity.
Purple	Can be creativity or fantasyland. You get to decide or ask which fits.
White	Pure, clean, a "Yes" to life, a blank page on which to write the next chapter.
Beige	Simplicity, a fairly neutral color. It doesn't make much of a statement, bland.
Yellow	Sunshiny, happy if the answer comes from a young person. Yellow can mean knowledge and thinking if the person is more mature.

What Is Your Floor Like?

"You're standing here. Your wall is over there. Look down. What do you see? What are you standing on?" Generally people are standing on rugs, fur, carpet, grass, dirt, marble, wood, sand, water, or rocks. This represents their support in life and their nurturing. You can tell how well nurtured they are by the nature of the material, the texture and by their description. It can also represent how much nurturing they are able to take in. The color of the floor or carpet or dirt can be interpreted using the same meanings described above. Let's look at some examples of responses to, "What are you standing on?" and my comments about their possible meanings.

"A beautiful mosaic wood floor. It looks good, but it's not real warm. Also it's very clean." Her life was very formal in appearance but lacked warmth and empathy. She kept her floor clean and kept her life looking good.

"Clay dirt that's brownish red." This floor is about old anger, and the person with this floor is not well nurtured, but things can still grow in it.

"The floor is hardwood." A hardwood floor has no softness. I wouldn't want to fall down on this floor!

"A desert scene with plants that don't die if you don't water them." This woman didn't have enough energy left in her to nurture anything else. It was pretty "arid" in her life and in her relationships.

"Brown carpet." The person with this floor has soft nurturing in her life as represented by the carpet, but she also has a functional life. Remember that brown is the color of doing.

"Cement." This is a cold and prison-like floor. It's very hard, and not pretty and not soft.

"Cold, wet, dirt floor. It's definitely not dusty." This is a very unattractive and non-nurturing floor. Wet seems to be important to this person, because wet is even more uncomfortable than a dusty dirt floor.

"Quicksand." This floor speaks of something which looks safe but isn't. For some reason the support this person has is treacherous and can be withdrawn or disappear at any moment.

"Shifting sands, like with the tides." This floor was described by a preadolescent male who was transferred back and forth from one parent to the other; with the rules changing each time he changed households.

"Sand, which is warm and dry. It's shifting, not solid." This floor was described by a woman whose husband had just left, causing her to be her own support system. The shifting sand represented the shift in support from her husband to herself.

Other people find themselves standing on things like a pedestal, a box, a tiny step stool. As one woman explained, "I'm standing on a pedestal, its round and layered. My wish in life is to be special just one time." When asked who or what these supporting items might represent, patients have mentioned the name of an important person in their lives, a job, a volunteer position or a loving relative. Sometimes they are not consciously aware of who or what the support represents. When this happens, I don't press the issue. Frequently these same patients return the next week and identify the source of their support, as if it had filtered through to the surface during the interim.

When an adolescent, who was not happy with the relationship with her father, looked down to see what she was standing on, she replied that she was standing on nothing. It must be unsettling to look down and see nothing under your feet! It doesn't make logical sense, but it makes perfect emotional sense. Remember that this aspect of the "wall questions," (i.e. What are you standing on? Or when you look down, what do you see?) reflects the support and nurturing a patient has in her life. The young lady described above did not feel she had any support at all. While it may be true that her parents cared for her and were providing for her physical needs, her perception was that they were not there for her emotionally. By her creative answer she communicated the lack of support she felt in her life. Isn't it interesting that this answer is a response to a question that presupposes she will be standing on <u>something</u>!

She was not alone. Several others described similar footings. I spoke with one young man who had recently signed up for the Air Force and was departing in a few days. He didn't fit into this mother's life; his father worked second shift and maintained a fairly solitary life; and the young man was leaving for the unknown. So when asked, "What are you standing on?" his reply was, "Nothing and I feel like I'm going to fall through."

A woman, recently separated from her husband, felt she was standing at the top of a set of stairs and was afraid to take a step forward into nothingness. This was symbolic of her life because she was afraid to move forward, to make a decision or to take charge of her life. Another woman, who valued relationships and did not have a solid relationship in her life, was standing on "air – not much of anything." A third young woman described her wall as a fish net about five feet in diameter. The fish net was woven and the strands were a combination of reddish/mauve and off-white. When asked to look down to see what she was standing on, she described herself as suspended in mid-air and seeing nothing below her. Upon reflection, she decided that she was like a fish caught long ago. The net was not protecting her - instead it had her trapped. And the red and white colors in the net were old bloodstains, which had become washed out and faded over the years. This image helped her understand why she felt stranded, unsupported and powerless.

A young woman, whose boyfriend had turned her over to one of his friends to use sexually, described her floor as "nothing, a black pit, it's there but it's not frightening."

We might wonder why it isn't frightening. It's much like a dream state. Often we have strange things happen in our dreams, time out of sync, space strangely used, someone talking to us who has been dead for a long time. Our left brain does not step in and judge or evaluate and say, "Oh no, that can't be right, there is supposed to be a floor there," or "time can't warp like that," or "oh no – he's dead." We just accept the activity of the dream. So is it too, with these strange answers. The responses come from inside the person without censoring and without having to meet the logical requirements of the left-brain.

These descriptions are painful to hear because they are so lacking in love, nurturing and support. But with this information, people can work on building a support base. They can take steps to nurture themselves. If they are in therapy, they can use the relationship with the therapist as a starting place for building a supportive network. They can search out other people who will be supportive as well. To know what one needs is the beginning of creating a solution. To be aware of one's vulnerability and weaknesses is to describe the place where one can begin.

One professional described his floor as bare dirt ground, which he found distressing. Sometimes he would talk about a mayflower being present and he would cry. He didn't understand his distress and he didn't understand his response to the flower. When we talked about what the ground meant, that the bare dirt represented his lack of nurturing and his lack of emotional support, he went to work on building a more substantial base. Having decided that he wanted more of these qualities in his life, he became adept at creating what he needed for himself and he became more open to what was being offered by others. He took responsibility for his life and his support system. He is now standing on rich green grass with lots of spring flowers.

Let's review our information. The height of the wall equals anger; the thickness of the wall represents protection from hurt; the composition makes a statement about how protected people are or how vulnerable they are; the color describes their attitude toward life and what they are standing on represents the nurturing or support they receive or are open to.

That leaves two other questions, "Are there doors, windows or gates?" and "Are they open, closed or locked?" The doors, windows and gates indicate how open people are to others and who these people are. People can be very specific about who they'll let in. Many times they won't let anyone in due to painful experiences in their past. In cases such as these, the doors, windows and gates are locked for extra protection or there will be no openings at all. This indicates that there has been a major breach of trust.

If you're the person with no doors, windows or gates, take a look at your trust level. One way of doing this is to ask yourself the question, "On a scale of zero to ten, with zero being none and ten being a lot, what is your trust level?" The answer will give you a starting place and an awareness of that place. The building of trust will take courage.

"My wall is opaque and hard to see through. It's twelve to fourteen feet thick. There is one window that's easy to see through. It's for Karen."

"My wall is gray; it's tall as the Empire State Building. It's made of concrete blocks, solid side out. There's one door for my boyfriend."

"My wall is one inch thick. It's orange and taller than me. It's easy to break. There are no doors, windows or gates. I don't trust anyone anymore." This description was from a mature teenager whose mother had been her best friend until she became involved in a new relationship and broke up the family unit to be with this person. The young girl had lost her mother's friendship and the family unit at the same time. Notice the vulnerability expressed in the very thin wall and the loss of trust.

"My wall is red. It's as tall as can be and three or four inches thick. There's a gate but it's locked. No one can enter."

"My wall is red brick. It's fourteen to sixteen inches thick and up to the clouds. I can see through but no one can see in. There are no doors, windows or gates." This description was from an adolescent who's divorced parents continued to battle over visitation issues while the young man had never adjusted to the break-up of his home.

What is Your Ceiling Like?

The last question is, "What do you see when you look up?" Blue sky and light fluffy clouds are the norm and indicate that people see positive things beyond their current situation. Anything other than blue sky gives a glimpse of their future orientation. Gray clouds, overcast sky, thunderstorms all describe a lack of improvement or trouble ahead. A ceiling indicates their perspective that the situation will never change and that they are locked in.

I call the ceiling the "trained flea syndrome," taken from Zig Ziglar's book, <u>See You at the Top</u>. In his book Zig talks about how one trains fleas. First you put them in a Mason jar with a lid on the top. The fleas spend a lot of time jumping up and hitting their heads on the lid. Pretty soon you notice that they're jumping a half-inch short of hitting the lid. They're no longer hitting their heads. Pretty smart fleas you might say. But then, you take the lid off and they'll jump a half-inch short of where the lid was. They're stuck in that jar by their own training. People are like that too. If they describe a lid, dome or ceiling over their heads, they're announcing that they don't believe they'll ever get out. They've placed a ceiling on their expectations and stopped trying. When the person with the lid is my patient, I tell them about the trained fleas. It gives them a new way of looking at that ceiling or dome or "plastic that curls over and covers." It gets a message to their subconscious about things that block growth and which don't really have to be there. After all, it's all in their imagination and they can change what they can imagine!

"My wall is light blue. It's 7 feet tall, 8 inches thick and made of cement blocks. There are no doors, windows, or gates. And there's a cement cap when I look up." This was from a gentleman who had been laid off on disability for a combination of emotional and physical problems. He would never be able to return to work. He would never be in better physical health and he would never be able to rise above his current financial situation. Hence the cement cap. The pale blue represented his sadness, his lack of power and his desire for harmony in a home where his children were argumentative and overly demanding of him.

"My wall is big and red. It's one foot thick, made of semi-blocks. There's one door that I can open if I want to. The floor is cement. When I look up I can't see the top. I feel closed in." This was from a young married woman who could see no way out of her difficulty.

"My wall is blue. It's five feet tall and four inches thick. It's made of bulletproof glass. There are no doors, windows or gates. The sky looks like it does when it storms, dark purple and blue gray." This from an adolescent male who's divorced parents fought constantly. He fought too, with them and with his peers in the neighborhood and in his school. Interesting, isn't it, that the color of his wall is blue, the color for harmony and security, the very things which have been destroyed for him and which he continues to destroy.

"My wall is black, tall, six feet thick. It's probably made of sticks because I can see faces through them. Sometimes it has doors, windows and gates, sometimes it doesn't. I'm standing on dirt and overhead are dark swirling clouds." This was from a young woman who had been physically and emotionally abused during her childhood. She had never resolved the pain of having no one to talk to - no one who cared about what was happening to her and the lack of physical or verbal affection in her life. Although her wall is very thick, she has no protection from the people in her life. She can still see their faces. Her future does not look any better with the dark swirling clouds.

One of the most significantly limiting walls came from a very disturbed young woman who was paranoid and frightened. Her wall was underground. It was made of dark clay. In some places it was hollow and in other places it was solid. Sometimes someone threw a rope down to her, other times there was no rope. When she looked up, she could see light in a small window way up high. She later added that I was the rope she could see hanging down.

Another significantly limiting wall came from a young man who had been beaten and abused by his mother. His wall was black and very tall. It would take ropes and climbing equipment to get over it. It was made of cement and steel and had no doors, windows or gates. When he looked up, all was black as well. He described it as looking like a prison wall. Later he remembered that his parents had pointed out prisons during his childhood telling him he would probably end up behind those walls.

In each of these cases, knowing how individuals perceived their world and particularly their future, helped me to help them. Knowing the limitations they perceived gave me a place to start and an opportunity to make them aware of this information. We could then work together to lift those lids.

I mentioned that people could be very creative and very imaginative with their walls. The next four walls are excellent examples of this:

"I see a stained glass window that's all different colors, particularly rose, lavender and brown. Sometimes I can see out and sometimes I can't. It depends on the color I'm behind. The window is closed and opens out. It's not locked. There's sort of a fog at my feet and I can't see what I'm standing on. It's not very supportive; it's rather wobbly. This wall is bigger than I am, but when I look up I see blue sky with clouds." This young woman had left a career in law, which did not suit her. She had been depressed and in ill health for over a year. The rose color represented loving ability, the lavender a helping quality and the brown her basic doing. She had a variety of options open to her and a number of directions to proceed in but her footing was shaky and she couldn't see clearly where to go.

"My wall is pink. It has tall screens that are a kind of mesh. I can't get over it, but I can see through it and see out. People cannot see in. It's very light and airy. There is a door, which goes one way only. The floor is hardwood. The sky is blue." This was from a loving woman who was very open to others. Her home-life was not loving, as represented by the hardwood floor. She had one door, opening out, which she was not ready to use yet.

"My wall is split in half. One half is black with red mean-looking faces. It's one foot thick and eight feet high. There's a thunderstorm when I look up and a bottomless pit when I look down. The other half is white, blue and yellow. It's one to two inches thick, and has a window for you (that's me, the therapist.) There are clouds with gold rays above and grass at my feet." A troubled teenager explained to me that the dark half described times of temper, emotional turmoil and family discord. The bright side described times of emotional balance, feelings of love and openness to learning.

"My wall is New England fieldstone. It's three feet high and two feet thick. I can climb over it easily. There are vines on it that are positively lovely. It winds forever with beautiful trees and grass and blue sky." This was from a very happy and fulfilled woman who had resolved many of the problems in her life.

I mentioned at the beginning of this chapter that sometimes it is interesting to see what you get when you ask, "And is there anything special about your wall?" One time I asked and the answer was, "Yes, there's a bird's nest on my wall and the baby bird is about to be pushed out." This came from a young woman who was creating turmoil in her parents' home and who was no longer wanted there. She felt very much like the baby bird that was being pushed from the nest.

As a final example, I'd like to tell you of the wall that changed the most. I often use a patient's wall as a barometer to determine progress during treatment and I suggest they continue to check their own progress when they're not seeing me. A 30-year-old gentleman had a wall that was white and three to four inches thick. It was made of plaster with metal and mesh in between, very strong and impenetrable. It was ten feet high with no doors, windows or gates. There was a gap between the wall and the ceiling. There also was a tile floor, which he described as old and often waxed. During the course of treatment we would periodically check on the condition of his wall. As he worked on himself, his wall began to change. It evolved so that it was made of cement bricks instead of metal and the ceiling had holes in it "like an iceberg melting." The wall continued to get lower, chest level, indicating more openness. The bricks hollowed out, indicating less vulnerability and less need to protect himself. The old waxed tiles were being torn up and a newly brushed concrete floor showed underneath. The new floor was not warm and nurturing but we felt the old tiles stood for family rules and societal "shoulds." The new floor was like a clean slate for him. The ceiling came down like an acoustical tile ceiling that could be replaced. When last seen, the acoustical tiles were gone and there was a lot of open space, symbolizing the end of the ceiling and opportunity for new growth.

Now, go back and look at your responses.

How tall is your wall? The response you gave will indicate the amount of anger that you feel. The taller the wall, the greater the anger. The lower the wall, the more open and trusting you are.

What is your wall made of? The more solid the material the greater the protection needed. Is your wall cement, steel or bulletproof glass? These indicate substantial need for protection. Is it made of a fragile material and will it break easily? Perhaps your wall does not give you enough protection. Can you see through your wall? Is it one-way glass? Sometimes people can see out but not let others see in. It often feels safer to see and not be seen. Is your wall soundproof? What does this mean in terms of your life? What have you had to hear that you didn't want to? What do you not want to hear now?

What color is your wall? When you check the list of colors, what does the interpretation mean? Does this color and its meaning fit with you and your attitude toward your life? Does it provide you with some information that you didn't have before? Is your wall a color that is not mentioned? Can you come up with an interpretation that seems to fit?

Are there doors, windows or gates? If so, are they open, closed or locked? What do the answers to these two questions tell you about your trust level? Are you trusting or not? What reasons might you have for not trusting? Why might your windows be locked? Who might a window or door be open for? Who do you trust in your life? How might you go about building greater trust? Where might you start with more trusting? Take a moment to write this down next to responses at the beginning of the chapter.

When you look down, what are you standing on? Is it solid or shifting? Is it something you can see or is it a sense of nothingness? What does the texture of this flooring tell you about the nurturing in your life? Is it representative of the nurturing provided or is it representative of what you can take in? What color is this flooring? What does this color tell you about the nurturing and support in your life? If what you're standing on is an object, who or what might that object represent? How do they support you in real life? Write this down too.

When you look up what do you see? Is it sunny and blue sky? Is it gray and cloudy? Do you have a lid or ceiling of some kind? What does this answer tell you about how you see your future? Are you optimistic or pessimistic? Do you believe that your world will ever change, will ever be better than it is right now?

Is there anything special or interesting or different about your wall? If so, what does it tell you about you? What meaning might it have about your life? Again, write the responses down next to your earlier observations.

There is no good wall or bad wall. There is nothing wrong with any of your answers. The answers come from inside of you and reflect your experiences. These are answers from you, to you, about yourself. They are not permanent answers. Your wall can change. It will change as you change. If you go to work on yourself, you will notice that your wall will change too.

What are some of the things you can work on? You can work on changing your self-talk. You can begin to monitor your thoughts. You can build a support system. You can increase your ability to trust. You can be sensitive to how you and your life are different now, as opposed to your childhood. You can begin to be aware of how old defenses no longer serve your needs. You can make changes and your wall will reflect them.

Personal Notes

Questions:

Thoughts:

Actions:

Chapter 3:
Who's Walking Around In Your Head With Muddy Boots?

Who's Walking Around In Your Head With Muddy Boots?

This chapter is about negative thoughts. Not what somebody else thinks about us, but the negative thoughts that we have about ourselves. We all have them, you know. Most people have some negative phrase they say to themselves on a regular basis. "I can never do anything right." "I'm stupid." "I never get what I want." "Why does this always happen to me?" "Good guys finish last." "It's lonely at the top." "It's too good to be true." "I don't deserve this." "I must not have been good enough."

We carry negative thoughts about everything - ourselves, how we look, our success, relationships, wealth, and life. For each of these areas (and many more) we have sayings or beliefs that limit us or control us. It is helpful to discover exactly what these beliefs are. Perhaps, by completing the next few sentences, you will get to become aware of some of your negative thoughts and sayings. If I provide the beginning of a sentence, see if you have a standard answer that you use to complete it.

The reason why I can't succeed is because

_____

_____

The reason why I'm so fat, thin, or ugly is because

_____

_____

The reason I have a bad (or no) relationship is because

_____

_____

I don't like my looks because

_____

_____

The problem with wealth is

_____

_____

What's your favorite negative thought about yourself?

_____

_____

Sometimes this negative phrase is a tape of someone else's words that we still play in our head. The words could have been said by parents, a brother or sister, a neighbor. Sometimes the messages were non-verbal - a look, a glare, a shrug of the shoulders, a rolling of the eyes, a sigh. This message, said by a significant person in our lives, was not questioned in any way. We were children and there was no way we could judge the accuracy of the message. We took it in, believed it and never questioned its accuracy. Now that we're older and wiser, we still play that tape. The messages from the tape get in the way of our being successful and they get in the way of our being happy.

What tape or message is still playing in your head?

_____

_____

A third way of understanding negative thoughts is to identify the character in our head that's saying all these negative things. This character can be someone real or something imaginary. The one constant is its ability to be negative and critical. I learned about the internal negative voice the hard way and the most significant way. I experienced it. I had a Loch Ness monster that I named "Nessie." This was a long time ago, before I had a graduate degree and even before I became a psychotherapist. Nessie would raise her ugly head and take advantage of every moment of my vulnerability. Actually, Nessie wasn't really ugly. Nessie would raise her head and begin to speak ugly thoughts, "You're not good enough" or "You're not smart enough." "You're too old to go back to school." "You'll never succeed." "You'll never be happy." Nessie was articulate and knew just when to speak up. Let there be a fleeting moment of doubt, a moment of weakness or loss of courage and Nessie jumped right in with a comment of her own. Of course, these comments were always on the negative side, the side determined to make me feel worse.

Times of change and times of newness were particularly difficult for me. I did pretty well with structure and familiarity, but if I were put in a new situation with unfamiliar skills or lack of expertise, my mind became fertile ground for Nessie's comments. So there I was, at the end of a marriage, in the middle of an awkward dating situation and beginning graduate school after a ten-year hiatus from college. Nessie rose up out of the Loch and had a lot to say.

I can't tell you just when I identified Nessie, or named her, but I distinctly remember when I took up the battle with the monster inside my head. The first time I told Nessie to "Shut up," she looked shocked! She turned her head toward me and looked at me in amazement. How dare I speak to her in such a manner? How could I possibly suggest that she be quiet? Nessie was quite distressed and not at all pleased. How dare I restrict her? Thus began the battle for the territory I called "my head."

I knew Nessie was part of me, but she certainly felt like and sounded like a separate entity. In any case, it was time I took control and since she was part of me I should be able to control her. Right? Wrong! Nessie had a mind of her own and a determination that would put most of us to shame. She did not intend to give up. She knew that if she was silenced she would lose power and possibly existence. She didn't want to do that! Nessie fought back. She took every opportunity to offer negative suggestions, encourage doubt, place obstacles and reasons why things wouldn't work out or life would never get better.

I battled back with "Shut up!" or "Be quiet" and "Go away;" anything to interrupt the flow of words, the negative comments, the castings of doubt. Nessie looked surprised and sometimes disdainful, but there would be brief, successful moments of silence. I came to cherish these moments and I gave myself great credit.

Awareness of Nessie increased and with this awareness the growing comprehension of the extent of her negativity and power over me. I became acutely aware that Nessie took a bad mood and made it worse, took a mild depression and plunged it deeper, took pangs of anxiety and turned them into a panicky pounding heart. I didn't like having my thoughts and moods out of my control, so I took charge and reclaimed my head. Eventually she began to subside. She would slide down into the water of the Loch and there would be blissful silence for a little while. But as soon as I wasn't looking, she would sneak a peak and begin her ascent. I'd turn on her and give her a verbal scolding, which sent her back down. Sometimes I heard her whispering, as if she were hidden behind a rock or a bush. She thought if I couldn't see her that she could get away with it. Gradually, I subdued her, quieted her running mouth and won control of the territory. She slipped quietly into the Loch.

Years later, when I thought her permanently submerged, Nessie nudged her head against the surface of the water and suggested a thought, very quietly, of course, just to see if I was receptive. Nessie is still out of sight but not out of mind. I'm well aware that she lurks nearby waiting for an opportune moment to reappear. She hasn't had the opportunity or invitation for a very long time.

Others writers have talked about their monsters. Susan Jeffers in <u>Feel the Fear and Do It Anyway</u>, calls it the Chatterbox. Richard D. Carson calls his the Gremlin and has addressed an entire book to <u>Taming Your Gremlin</u>. He also notes that you can call your monster anything you wish – the Grim Reaper, the General, the Coach, or Big Ugly. This book is particularly good for male readers. Paula Butler in <u>Talking to Yourself</u> labels the various aspects of the self-dialogue as the Driver, the Stopper and the Confuser. All three of these books are excellent resources on this subject and I highly recommend them.

Having been victorious in my battle, I wanted to give my patients the power to control what went on in their minds. I wanted them to win the battle for supremacy of their thoughts. I wanted to give them tools they could use in good times and in bad, whether I was there or not. I began by asking for a positive and a negative symbol to represent themselves. What I was really asking was for them to identify that side of themselves which had nothing good to say about them. I was looking for a name or label for their Loch Ness monster.

There was a young woman, in her late teens, who had lost her mother and was now living with her father and brother. The father was an alcoholic who treated her badly. In turn she then selected boyfriends who treated her as her father had. She didn't think she was worth much to people. She didn't feel she had any rights. Her self-esteem was low and her sense of power was even lower. She couldn't see that her life was ever going to change or become any better. She had a lot to say to herself and most of it was negative.

During sessions we tried a number of tactics to reduce the emotional pain, to increase her sense of power and to improve her outlook. Nothing worked. My therapy was like a Band-aid - supportive but not healing, caring but not curing. Then one day we talked about symbols, about identifying a positive and a negative symbol to work with. She grasped the idea quickly and came up with symbols, which had meaning for her. Her positive symbol was a pine tree in the moonlight - tall, stately, graceful and strong. Her negative symbol was a Troll - a short, fat, ugly Troll wearing dark green clothes. She described where he lived and talked about his nasty disposition. We looked at his effect on her, how he encouraged her negative thoughts and depressed her mood, how he encouraged her to feel badly about herself and not worthy of correct treatment or loving care. I suggested she listen to what he was saying, not try to change anything, but just listen for the first week.

She left that session with a new sense of awareness. She went out and bought trolls of every size and description. She bought pictures of trolls and ceramic trolls and books about trolls. She placed these all around her bedroom to remind her of his presence. Then she listened. She listened to what he had to say and when he said it. She noted how she felt when he talked and she didn't like it at all.

When she returned a week later, she was feeling better about herself. She'd become familiar with the monster in her head and was acutely aware of the damage he was doing. We talked about the struggle that was ahead of her, how she would have to do battle with her Troll for control of her head and control of her thoughts. I told her of my battle with Nessie. I told her about the words I'd used to squelch Nessie and the strong power I'd been up against. She understood that this was not going to be easy.

Two weeks later she returned, feeling wonderful. She glowed with power and energy. There was a spring in her step and the young woman who had felt browbeaten and unworthy was nowhere to be seen. I asked what had made the difference, what had changed. "I've got Troll control!" she proudly announced.

The next step was how to maintain this "Troll Control." Our minds don't stay positive by themselves. They require constant and consistent care, much like teeth require consistent brushing. What happens when you don't brush your teeth? They get skuzzy. They get yellow. The tartar builds up. The gums decay and cavities appear. Our minds are the same way. If we don't "brush them," they get skuzzy. They get negative. They get full of doubts and fears. So we have to attend to our mind on a daily basis and be aware of who is talking and what's being said. We have to get and maintain "Troll Control."

And how do we control those negative thoughts that flow through our minds? How do we control them, whatever name we give to them or however pervasive they have become? First, become aware that they exist. Becoming aware of the thoughts that go though our head is the most difficult task of all. After all, we've been hearing these words most of our life. They sound just fine to us; like normal, everyday talk. We even think they make sense! What we're not aware of is the extent of the negativity. This negativity inhibits us and puts obstacles in our paths. Yet we stick to it for a familiar sense of security. As negativity grows so does the character's control in your head. Its plan is to keep you where you are. It is insidious.

I had the occasion to ride in the car with a dear friend who had always seemed very pleasant and very positive. Imagine my surprise when I heard her say to herself, "Can't you do anything right? You should have known better than that, you dummy you." She was only pulling out of the driveway! To her, this self-talk was normal. To me it was a dialogue of put-downs. She wouldn't dream of talking to anyone else in this manner, but she thought of speaking to herself this way. She didn't hear the negativity. Sometimes the general conversation in our heads is negative. Sometimes it's a full-fledged monster. Either way, don't put yourself down for having this negativity. Do something about it! Become aware of *who* is saying *what* in your head. Listen for the negative comments and the criticism; begin to know that you can control what goes on in your head.

So, awareness is the first step. Getting some leverage is the second step. In physics, leverage is the ability to lift more than your weight with the assistance of a lever. On Wall Street, leverage is the ability to buy more stocks with less money. In psychotherapy, leverage is the extra power needed to motivate yourself for change. Leverage is the desire, the determination to want change. You have to want this for yourself and you have to believe that it can happen. So get determined. Get leverage. Want something better for yourself.

How? Get angry. Get irate. How dare someone make you miserable! How dare someone walk around in your head with muddy boots! How dare someone talk to you this way? Get angry! Get back by getting rid of it! Do it now!

Put a label on it or discover its name. Figure out what it looks like and where it lives. What havoc does it like to wreak in your life? What's it stopping you from doing? What doubts does it put in your mind? What does it have to say when you're worried, or scared, or about to venture into something new? What does it have to say about the relationship you're in? What does it say about your worth? And what does it say about what you deserve in the future?

Decide once and for all that its word is not the gospel truth. You don't have to believe it and you don't have to limit yourself. There was a time, when you were a child, that you had no doubts or fears. You tried walking, and people laughed at you when you fell down, but you kept on trying and eventually you walked. What happened to that innate sense of adventure and striving, of eagerly trying new things, of risk taking? Where did it go?

It went down the road, or was hidden like a treasure along with the other child-like qualities you possessed when you began to take in statements from those around you. I'll bet you heard "no" 40,000 times as a child and "yes" maybe 2,000 times. In addition, to the "no," you probably also heard, "You can't do that, you're too little," or "It will never work." Or worse, you might have been told that you are dumb or stupid. You might have been told that girls aren't smart or that boys don't show their feelings. Big people told you this and you believed them. You took all of these statements in and decided they knew best. If someone important to you scowled, you decided that you'd done something wrong and would never do that again. If someone important to you was in a bad mood, you assumed it was because of something you'd done wrong and you may have taken that in as a message about your behavior too. So these statements grew. These statements that talked about your worth, value, talents and skills were internalized as absolute truths. These messages are still there, loud and strong, ready to comment on your every action and reaction as an adult. These statements are ready to judge, evaluate and find you wrong. They are ready to tell you not to try something because you're too big, or too old, or too short, or the wrong gender. Just fill in the blank. You don't know these words are limiting you because you've heard them all your life.

So now as you hear the words, hopefully, you're beginning to recognize these statements as untrue and definitely not in your best interest. You've got awareness! Secondly, you've got leverage. You don't want these thoughts anymore. You're determined to take over, to take control of what goes through your head. You're going to stop that person from walking around in your head with muddy boots.

How, exactly, are you going to do this? One of the ways is to interrupt the pattern. I used an expletive to interrupt the pattern with Nessie. I told her to, "Shut up and leave me alone!" You can tell your thoughts to "Shut up!" "Go away!" or "Get lost!" Choose whatever is comfortable for you. Fight back with your words and with your own power. Don't let somebody else's words determine what you're going to say about yourself or to yourself. Interrupt the pattern of these thoughts. Do it now.

Not only can you talk back, but you can use your creative imagination to silence this talking monster. You could think of closing a door on it or hanging up the phone. You could encourage it to take a hike, to go for a swim, to go under the bridge and stay there. You could tape its mouth shut. You could imagine it in a cage. You could put up a piece of soundproof glass between the two of you. You could put yourself in a soundproof room designed to isolate you from the sound of its voice. Whatever comes to mind is yours to use!

A third way to take control is to change the radio station. You know how radio stations tell you to stay on that spot on the dial? They know if you move to another spot, you won't be able to hear their station. You can't listen to two radio stations at the same time. Our minds are the same way. We can't listen to two stations, two speakers in our head at that same time. Change that dial! Move to a different idea; think a different thought. Remember a time on an island or the ocean that was idyllic. Remember a time when you felt powerful and proud. Remember a time when someone recognized your talent. Remember a time when you succeeded. Remember a time when you felt happy.

If remembering is not your strong suit, take action to change the radio station. Go to the mirror and make a funny face. Go to a movie or go out and rent a movie. Bake cookies, bread or pies. Take those goodies to a neighbor or a shut-in; take them to a mommy who works all day and doesn't have time to bake. Do something nice for someone not as fortunate as yourself. Find places to volunteer your time so you'll be busier and your mind will have other things to think about. Dig in the garden, work in the yard, plant flowers or trim bushes. Do something active like play golf or tennis, go hiking or horseback riding. Ride your bike, whether it is an exercise bike, a mountain bike or a motorcycle. Find a river for rafting. Or, do something you have been putting off - organize a closet, straighten the garage or clean the basement. My philosophy behind this is, as long as you're miserable, you might just as well do something you don't like to do. Amazingly enough, you'll end up feeling productive.

Learning to calm your mind is both ages old and new thought, as well. It goes by the name meditation. The instructions are to find yourself a quiet place where you won't be disturbed. Then sit quietly, either with your eyes focused on one thing, like a candle, a flower, a crystal; or closed with no image in front of them. Let your mind roam or wander, and then gently bring it back to the peacefulness of "no thought." Encourage it and allow your mind to be still. Give your head the experience of utter peacefulness. For beginners, it is a wonderful experience in learning the beginnings of peacefulness and mental quiet. For persons experienced in meditating, it is a wonderful opportunity to nurture themselves with silence, to hear their inner wisdom and to get answers for the day's challenges. It is something you can try on your own or find a group where this practice is taught.

There are many books on this subject: Shakti Gawain's <u>Creative Visualization</u> and <u>Living in the Light,</u> Louise Hay's <u>You Can Heal Your Life</u> and <u>The Power is Within You</u>, Martin Rossman's <u>Healing Yourself</u> and Joan Borysenko's <u>Minding the Body, Mending the Mind</u> to name just a few. These are some of the books I've used and there are many more available at your library or bookstore.

Another way to change the radio station is to learn the skill of breathing. Attend an aerobics class or seek out a yoga class. There you will learn how to breathe in different ways. (You may have thought there was only one way to breathe, in and out. You have much to learn!) As you learn to concentrate on your breathing and to change how you breathe, you'll notice that you have also changed that spot on your radio dial. There is also the very basic controlled breathing method for immediate use as an antidote to negative thoughts or strong negative emotions. Breathe in to the count of five, hold for the count of five, and release slowly to the count of five. Do this five times and notice how you have interrupted the previous thought pattern. Notice that you're thinking about counting and breathing, not about whatever thought was causing you distress. The breathing calms you and the counting distracts your mind. You can do this anytime, anywhere.

The most extreme example of changing the radio station and changing her thoughts was accomplished by a young woman who went bungee jumping. She was plagued with self-destructive thoughts. She said the bungee jumping had the same element of self-destructiveness, but it could be done safely. It was the only way she could take her mind off self-destructive thoughts and she said it was successful. I'm sure skydiving would accomplish the same thing.

Take charge of your life. Take charge of your thoughts. Be creative. Do something different and then reward yourself.

Reward yourself for *any* progress. This means, if you have five minutes less chatter, praise your new control. If you have an hour of blissful thoughts, pat yourself on the back. Give yourself credit for any progress that moves you in the direction you want to go. Understand this is a battle. You fight for inches, not miles. You fight for minutes, not days and weeks. You work to win each skirmish, no matter how seemingly insignificant it may be. Contrary to what our parents believed and taught us, we will not get "swelled heads" by praising ourselves. Actually we will become more loving and have more to give to others.

Some examples are provided here, since many of us did not experience a lot of positive reinforcement as children.

"Good job, well done."
"Wow, you did great!"
"Atta girl."
"You did it, you shut him up."
"Keep up the good work."
"Bravo!"
"Outstanding."
"You're catching on."
"Nothing can stop you now."
"You're fantastic."
"I knew you could do it."
"You figured it out."
"Good for you."
"Nice work."
"Way to go."
"Hurray for you."

You must understand the battle is never really over. The culprit, the foe, the monster, is just over the next ridge waiting for you to turn your back. She'd like you to forget she's there. She waits for you to ease your vigilance, for you to let down your guard. She thinks she can slip in when you're not looking and when you're not listening. She's right. She can! So you need to beware, even when the major portion of the battle is over. She's there, ready to put in a word about the times it didn't work, or how you're really not good enough, or how you don't deserve to have these good things in your life. The list is endless and your vigilance needs to be constant. Be thoughtful about your thoughts. Get Troll Control!!!

Workbook Page

Who's walking around in your head with muddy boots?
_____

Does it have a name? What is it?
_____

How would you describe this character, this monster?
_____

What are some of its favorite things to say to you?
_____

When are your most vulnerable times?
_____

Give me one reason why it shouldn't be here. (We're looking for leverage.)
_____

What are your best defenses against its negative talk?
_____
_____

List three things you can do or say to shut up your monster.

_____

_____

_____

How will you know when you're winning the battle?

_____

What are three positive things you can say to yourself when the monster shuts up?

_____

_____

_____

Personal Notes

Questions:

Thoughts:

Actions:

Chapter 4:
What Color Is Your Aura?

What Colour Is Your Aura?

Ben, a wise 3½ year old, sat with me in the auditorium. We were watching his aunt parade though the ceremony that concluded two years of graduate school. I can't think why I asked the question, "Ben, do you see colors?" There was silence and his big eyes looked at me. He appeared unsure of my question or maybe it was not a safe question to answer. So I asked a different question,

"What color is Auntie Julie?"
"Red."
"What color is Mommy?"
"Brown."
"What color is Granny?"
"Green."
"What color is Grandpa?"
"Pink."
"What color is Baby Jacob?"
"White."

The colors Ben mentioned were not the colors of the clothes his family had on, nor was he was talking about the color of their eyes. My impression was that he spoke of the colors that surrounded the people in his family, their auras.

Auntie Julie was graduating from a master's program and had plans to start her own business. She had lots of energy and drive. She was an initiator and a motivator; people loved her enthusiasm. The color Ben saw around her was red.

Mommy was mother to three children under the ages of 3 ½ and she had a lot to get done. Brown is the color of doing. It's not a good color or a bad color; it's just the color of one who is focused on tasks. It was a very appropriate color for her.

Granny was a great teacher for Ben. She encouraged him to do things on his own, learn skills he'd need later in school and encouraged him to explore and try new things. Green is the color of independence and growth.

Grandpa loved Ben and played with him often. They'd romp and play in the living room and in the back yard. They'd play games and they'd play "pretend." It was always done in a loving manner. Pink is the color of love.

Baby Jacob was only three months old. The color Ben saw around him was white, the clean slate, the color of purity.

These colors, called auras, are the energy we radiate from our bodies. The quality of the color and the tone of color are determined by the thoughts we hold most often in our mind. You didn't know, did you, that what you feel and think about is out there, surrounding your body, for everyone to see! If you did know that, would it change how you think?

I had the opportunity to discover how it felt to have my thoughts known by someone else. Having been so successful in asking Ben the question about colors, I next asked a six-year-old client who seemed wiser than her years. "Randy, do you see colors?" Randy didn't say anything for a moment, but looked around me in a big arc two feet outside my body. I knew what she was looking at, so I wasn't surprised when she said, "Yes." "Well, what color am I?" I asked. "Oh, you're rainbows!"

I want to tell you what a wonderful feeling it is to have your aura described as "rainbows." It's flattering and reinforcing. I asked her what the colors of the rainbow meant. To her, pink was love, green was grass and Easter and good things, blue was "no fighting."

Because of the colors, she always knew when her Mommy was saying one thing and feeling another. Mommy was a single parent, struggling with the responsibility of raising two children and maintaining a job. Sometimes she felt overwhelmed and sometimes she felt angry. Oftentimes Mommy didn't want Randy or her younger sister to know how overwhelmed she felt, but Randy could always see what she was feeling. So Randy always knew when something was wrong and that was a big responsibility for a six year old.

One day Randy arrived for her session at the end of what had been a long, hard day for me. I was tired and just wanted to get the day over with. Unfortunately, or perhaps not so unfortunately, I asked Randy, "What color am I today?"

"Brown."

Oops! Nothing like being told your energy is task oriented, when you're in the business of healing, nurturing and empowering! I immediately began to work on my state of mind and on changing it. You can, you know. You can change what you're thinking and what you're feeling so you can change what colors people see in your aura.

We talked a lot about taking charge of our thoughts in the last chapter. In this chapter we're going to talk about changing our state of mind.

State of Mind Makes a Difference

Our state of mind is determined by what we focus on. *What we focus on expands.* What we focus on manifests in our auras. So, if we are focusing on lack, on things we don't have in our life, we'll feel lacking, needy and empty. Amazingly enough, everywhere we look we'll notice things we don't have in our lives. Then we'll begin to attract less of what we want or need.

If we focus on brown we'll see more brown in our lives. If we focus on doing, we will only notice the things we have to do and we will feel as if our nose is to the grindstone. If there is any martyrdom in us, we will notice how we are doing all the work and no one else is. Then we will feel anger, resentment, and self-pity. If we focus on getting shortchanged in life, we will notice each and every experience that could possibly represent being shortchanged. We will attract more experiences of this nature into our lives.

If we focus on positive things, such as having what we want in our lives, on our health, or on the beauty that surrounds us, then we will have an opportunity to feel blessed, to feel thankful, to feel gratitude. These feelings create more beautiful auras. That's one reason to change our state of mind. Positive feelings also make us feel better. That's another reason to change our state of mind. You've already learned how to control what you think, now control what you focus on. Then watch what you focus on expand.

A topic, which demonstrates this, is a trip to Belize that I took several years ago. Friends and I decided one summer that we wanted to go to the Mayan ruins near Belize for the Christmas holidays. We talked about Belize, we acquired maps of the area and we set up very tentative plans. Soon articles on Belize in magazines and newspapers jumped out at us. A friend called to say there was a television program on Belize on some channel at six o'clock that evening. Another friend mentioned that he'd done a medical missionary stint in that area. At a five-day workshop in Ohio, one of the participants was from an island near Belize. She heard about our desire to visit Belize, and invited us to come and stay at her guesthouse, and we did!

When we began to think about Belize, Belize began to be everywhere; it expanded. The more we thought about it, the more we brought Belize into our lives. It's a simple but very effective example.

When you get to the work page at the end of this chapter, you'll have an opportunity to write down what you think about, and what you'd like to have expanded in your life.

Colors Have Meaning

Now, back to colors and auras and what they mean. There seems to be a universality of meaning when it comes to color. Those who have studied auras have handed down these meanings. People who have studied healing with colors have talked about their meanings. Dorothee L. Mella just wrote a book entitled <u>The Language of Color</u>, Reverend Gloria Charlton taught a class on auras in Michigan, Frank Don wrote a book entitled <u>Color Your World</u>. What follows is drawn from a variety of sources. I've also expanded on the meanings based on my experiences and feedback from clients, especially the children.

Red is a very physical color. It means vitality and life energy. People with this color are strong-minded and strong-willed. They are ambitious and have a strong commanding nature with leadership abilities. They are brave, courageous and daring. They are generous and affectionate, attracting people with their magnetic personalities. They may have a materialistic outlook on life.

The darker, muddied shades of red can indicated negative emotions such as anger and rage. Do you recall the adage about "seeing red" when you're angry? The darker shades can also reflect lust, loudness and domination. This red may describe the loud, "bigger-than-life" sort of person that some tend to shy away from.

Orange stands for health and vitality. It is the color of activity and doing. People who have orange around them frequently are leaders, but without a lust for power. They lead by example. They are good managers and good social mixers; often they are the "live wires" of the party. Darker shades of orange indicate selfishness and pride.

Yellow symbolizes thought, intellect and mental concentration. It stands for wisdom and knowledge. Bright, optimistic people have yellow in their auras. They are intelligent and capable. Yellow also represents light, as in sunlight. Yellow chases away fear and worry, the negative thoughts which cloud the mind. Dark, dingy shades of yellow denote jealousy, suspicion and negative thinking.

Green stands for energy, individualism and growth. It is independence and freedom from bondage. It is new life. Think of a seedling sprouting up from the ground and growing. Green is often seen in the auras of people who are successful and prosperous. They have had lots of ideas and they consistently see them to fruition.

The negative aspects of green, when it's dark and dingy, are envy and jealousy. Do you remember the phrase, "green with envy?" This is the shade of green that's being referred to. Deceit and treachery are also in this color tone.

Blue represents self-reliance and confidence. Persons with blue in their aura have the positive characteristics of sincerity, idealism, and a harmonious nature. They are loyal friends. It can be the color of solitude, harmony and security. The negative aspects of blue are the darker colors, which indicate depression and sadness when harmony is missing from someone's life.

Indigo is the color of deep sincerity, integrity and inner wisdom. People with a high degree of spirituality and people of deep religious convictions have indigo in their aura. People of profound artistic talent, who stay tuned in to this gift, have indigo in their aura. Thus, it is also the color of creativity.

Violet, the soft shade of purple, is the color of contribution. People with violet in their auras are giving, sharing and caretaking. They give much and ask very little for themselves.

Brown is the color of organization and orderly management. It is the color of convention and perseverance. People with a brown aura are systematically getting the job done. Do not expect this person to be especially sensitive or emotional.

Gray is the color of convention and formality. Think of <u>The Man in the Gray Flannel Suit</u>. This is the person with the "red tape" mentality. There is a lack of imagination and creativity, but much persistence to get the job done in just the right manner. Thus, gray can indicate dullness. If it becomes dark, gray can denote meanness.

Pink and Mauve are the colors of love and caring.

White is the color for purity, cleanliness of mind, the clean slate and openness.

Finding Auras

There are lots of things that exist that we can't see – radio waves, television signals,

X-rays, violet and ultra-violet rays, infrared rays. There was a time when scientists and specialists didn't know these rays existed. They do now and can prove their existence. The same is true for auras. There was a time when scientists and specialists didn't know of <u>their</u> existence. They do now and can prove their existence with Kirlian photography. Every living thing has an aura – plants, trees, animals, people. The aura is the energy they emit, and that energy has a frequency and vibration that reveals itself in a color. Each color has a universal meaning. Amazingly enough, children know the meanings of these colors without ever being told.

I was working recently with a family of three small children ages six to ten. All three exhibited a knowledge of the meaning of colors, in different ways. The oldest could see auras and knew what they meant, the middle child couldn't see them but could describe the meaning of the different colors and the youngest child had just drawn a picture of mommy half pink and half dark blue. The pink stood for love and the blue stood for mother's misery and unhappiness.

Some people can see an aura easily. Others have to work to develop or reclaim the gift. I'm not sure if we all come into the world able to see auras and then lose the gift, or if some of us come into the world able to see auras and others don't. Randy sees colors, but her younger sister doesn't. One woman spoke of seeing colors around people when she was a child. Since no one else ever mentioned the colors, she didn't either. Sometime later, she doesn't know exactly when, she stopped seeing colors altogether. Another woman, who didn't know that auras existed and had never seen an aura, saw colors the moment she was told of their existence by someone she trusted.

One way I've described the "finding" of auras is to relate auras to a television station that you want to dial in. This dates back to the days when televisions were simpler and everything was manual. In those days you turned a dial in order to find or bring in a particular station. Auras are the same way. To find them, you need to turn the dial slightly until the aura comes into focus. And how do you do that?

I have people begin by looking at my head with a pale or neutral colored wall in the background. I tell them, "Just look at my head and then unfocus your eyes. Let your vision get blurry. Don't look exactly at me, that's traditional vision. Look at my head in an unfocused way. Gaze side-ways at my hair. Let the halo or arc of light around my head just appear." It's always surprising to experience this for the first time. If you go back and look again, with traditional vision, you'll notice that the aura goes away! So try again. Unfocus, look differently than you usually do and see what appears - often somewhat miraculously! Then look to the outside of the glow or halo of light and see if you can catch a glimpse of color. Believing that there is an aura and color helps this process.

Interestingly enough, one young woman who had a "lazy" left eye said she could see auras better with her left eye than she could with her right eye.

Sometimes I can see the halo of energy, sometimes I can't. Sometimes I can see color around people, sometimes I can't. It helps me if people are feeling an emotion strongly. This makes the aura bigger and easier for me to see. Other people can see auras all the time. I envy them!

What if you can't see colors around people? Tell me, have you ever walked into a room and sensed anger? Or felt sadness? Or had an intuitive feeling that someone was depressed without being told? Some people can feel the vibrations; can have knowingness about the colors without ever being able to see them. Are you one of those people who can sense when you're being told a lie? Have you ever let yourself down, felt in an instant that you'd failed, and sensed something about yourself deflating?

To give you an example, I will share a personal experience. I was to meet a friend in a parking lot before going into a seminar. She was frightened and had asked for my support. I agreed. I arrived at the seminar and parked in front of the building, totally forgetting about my commitment. I walked blithely into the seminar, not remembering that I was to join her and we were to walk in together. When she arrived, five minutes later, it all came back to me. I felt myself deflate. I was drained of energy as I realized the extent to which I had let someone down. I felt terrible. My aura crashed and burned. It was hours before I managed to reconstruct a decent energy level again. My aura had deflated because of what I said to myself at that moment. I had broken my word. I had let someone down. The responsibility was mine. The fault was mine. My thoughts were negative and critical. Now I know that this may not seem like a big thing to you, but in breaking my word, I had gone against my value system. The thoughts affected my feelings and thus affected my entire body; my aura deflated in response.

In a hospital, notice the difference in energy emitted by the nursing staff and yourself, as compared with the patients. Healthy people generally have good energy. Patients generally do not. Their energy level is usually depleted due to illness or injury and their thoughts about their condition. When my son was hospitalized for two weeks following a car accident, our family spent ten to twelve hours a day with him. We often talked about how we had to lower our energy level to be in his room. Then, when we left at night, we'd work to reclaim our energy so we could feel fully alive once again.

People with strong feelings emit strong colors. If the feelings are healthy and positive, the colors reflect this meaning. If the feelings are intensely negative or angry, the colors reflect this meaning too.

One lady, slightly past middle age, was very unhappy about her life situation. She was married to an alcoholic who controlled and spoiled her life. She had allowed him to do this for years and was just beginning to claim her power and her rights. I had to talk for weeks to get this feeling of empowerment started! As she became empowered, she began to feel angry. One particular day in my office, I began to unfocus, and I saw red like a blazing fire all around her. I looked again, the traditional way, and the red went away. This is the part I described as dialing in a television station. If you turn the dial too far, you get static; but if you turn the dial just right, you get a clear picture. So I unfocused again, looking side-ways at her, and there was the red again. Her face looked like there were blazing coals underneath, reflecting upon her skin. It was simply amazing. I told her what I saw and I told her the possible meaning of the color red. My interpretation was that she was feeling great anger; she confirmed that interpretation.

Another time I had the opportunity to give someone a very special gift, a gift of love and "knowingness." Wanda is a person who had fought depression for years. She could no longer work. She had no friends in her life and no energy to attract friends. She only had her family, her children and her grandchildren, and she gave much to them. Guess what color I saw around her head and shoulders as she talked about her family? It was a very pale purple, the color we call violet. I really didn't want to scare her with this information, because I wasn't sure how she'd receive it. So, knowing that she attended church regularly and being familiar with the intensity of the religious services she attended, I asked if she had ever noticed glowing circles around the heads of the congregation during the service. She had. She didn't know what they were, but she had sometimes noticed halos of light around people's heads. I told her that the glowing was a good thing, that it meant people were thinking good thoughts and praying strongly. Then I gave her the gift; I told her about the pale purple aura about her head. I told her it meant she was a giving, caring person who does for others and gives more than she ever receives. She left my office that day with a gift, a gift *from* herself, *to* herself. She left with the knowledge that she was a giving person, a person who contributed much to the lives of others, and that she had this in her aura for all to see.

Seeing, Non-Traditionally

So, let's review how you begin to see auras. First, you need to believe they exist. You can take my word for it, you can read about them, or you could try this exercise. Have someone with a strong energy level sit in a chair facing away from you. Stand behind them with your eyes closed and bring your hands slowly down toward their hair. You should feel something "cloudlike" anywhere from 3 to 8 inches away from their head. It's a very subtle feeling, like there are cotton balls around their head. If you can feel this cloud or sense of cotton balls, which is really their aura or their energy field, you are more apt to believe that there is something you can see.

Learn to unfocus; learn to look differently, in a non-traditional way, in order to see an aura. It's a lot like looking out the side of your eyes. See what you can "tune in" by doing this. Then look directly at an aura or halo and see what happens. Does it go away, like it does for me?

Practice on household pets, practice on people. Have them hold still, with a neutral colored wall behind them and practice looking in an unfocused sort of way. The first thing you're apt to see is a glow of energy or halo effect. Practice seeing it, then practice tuning it out. I figure if you can tune it out, then you can also learn to tune it back in. As you become a believer of energy glowing about the head, you're more apt to begin picking up colors around people. Then begin looking at the whole body and watch for energy and color there.

Use lectures, speaking engagements, workshops, and classrooms as places to practice seeing auras. People who are projecting their voices and their personalities are apt to be emitting strong feelings and therefore vivid, seeable auras. One workshop presenter had a beautiful blue aura around him for two days. He was teaching peace, harmony and oneness. Another teacher, who was instructing college students thinking about starting their own businesses, had a lovely golden aura about him each class period. He was thoughtful about his work and dedicated to teaching how to think in order to be successful too.

Try to catch a glimpse of your own aura. This can get very creative. When you're standing in the shower and it's steamy, look at your feet in an unfocused sort of way. What can you see? Or look in the steam-covered mirror when you get out of the shower. Don't wipe it off, leave it just as it is and look above your head, in an unfocused sort of way, while you dry your hair. Do you see a halo of light around your head? Have you ever caught some color out of the corner of your eye, by your hands perhaps? This is your aura, the color of your thoughts and attitude at that moment.

You might also notice areas of color projected onto the paper where you're writing. You might notice blotches of color on a wall that you're staring at without realizing it. By looking indirectly, in that unfocused way, you can see spots of color. I believe this is a projection of you aura, what some ancients called "thought forms." The color of the projected spots, or thought forms, matches the color of your aura. The day my real estate agents announced the sale of my house, a day I had been anticipating for six months, I projected the brightest mass of green everywhere I looked. I was happy and I was free to pursue my dream!

You can make your aura bigger by expanding your feelings, by projecting stronger feelings. Have you ever returned from a workshop feeling bigger and stronger than you ever had before? There was a reason for this. After the workshop you were projecting a bigger volume of energy. You returned feeling loved, valued and purposeful. All of these feelings were greatly empowering, and they were all reflected in your aura.

You can change the color of your aura by changing the thoughts that go through your head. If you are feeling negative emotions like depression, disappointment or sadness, your aura is going to reflect this. If you are feeling angry, irritated, frustrated, mad or raging, your aura is going to reflect this emotion in its color. People can feel what you're feeling. Some people can "see" what you're feeling. Your aura cannot lie. It always tells the truth about you. What do you want people to see and know about you? What do you want people to feel from you?

On the workbook pages that follow, you will have an opportunity to answer questions related to auras and experiences you may have had with them. You'll also have an opportunity to answer questions about what thoughts you wish to hold most often in your mind.

Workbook Page

Do you remember seeing color around a person when you were a child?

_____

When did you stop seeing this color?

_____

Have you ever noticed a glow around someone's head?

_____

As an adult, have you ever noticed color around a person or in places where you never expected to see color?

_____

What did you say to yourself about what you saw?

_____

Can you think of something else, maybe kinder, to say about it?

_____

Have you ever noticed color around yourself?

_____

Where were you, or when or how did you see color around yourself?

_____

Have you ever wondered about auras and what they meant?

_____

Does knowing about auras and the meaning of the colors giving you a reason for managing your thoughts and feelings? Why?

_____

What kind of thoughts and feelings do you generally hold about what happens to you?

_____

What thoughts and feelings do you generally hold about what you have in your life?

_____

What kind of thoughts and feelings do you generally hold in you head about lack and abundance?

_____

How often do you think in terms of gratefulness about your health, your life, those who love you, or the beauty that surrounds you?

_____

What do you give thanks for each day?

_____

In what ways do you feel that you are lucky or blessed?

_____

_____

What one thing would you like to have expanded in your life?

_____

What is one reason for changing what you think about?

_____

What is one way you can change your state of mind?

_____

Personal Notes

Questions:

Thoughts:

Actions:

Chapter 5:
How Clean Are Your Windows?

How Clean Are Your Windows?

"Better keep yourself clean and bright; you are the window through which you must see the world." (George Bernard Shaw) What is interesting is that you often view the world through a distorted piece of glass, unknowingly, of course. Decisions made in childhood and early adolescence affect the window through which you see the world. These decisions were made unconsciously and continue to operate at an unconscious level. They cause you to distort what you see and what you hear. They determine what you will let into your life and what you will exclude. These unconscious decisions are usually about trust, love and worthiness. If you don't feel you are loveable, then you cannot let in love. If you don't feel you deserve good things, then you will not allow good things to come into your life. If you don't trust others, then you will not trust someone to love you. If you feel you have no value, then you will act in such a way as to prevent value from coming into your life. You become so accustomed to these beliefs that you never question them. Actually, you believe them because you've heard them for so long!

In order to free yourself from the limitations of these decisions, it is first necessary to become aware that they exist.

One way to do this is take some quiet time for yourself when you won't be disturbed and go back through a series of childhood memories with your eyes closed. Look at the incidents that took place and ask yourself, "What decision did I make about myself at that time?" "What did I say to myself about love?" "What did I say to myself about trust?" "What did I say to myself about being important?" "How did I explain to myself the treatment I received from my parents or my brothers and sisters?" Listen to yourself for phrases you use most often. "I'm not important." "Nobody ever listens to me." "I must not be loveable." "I never do anything right." "I have to be perfect or they won't love me." "I don't deserve good things." These and other decisions like them rule your life at a subconscious level. They operate in your life, whether they are appropriate or not. Usually there is one outstanding decision that is more powerful than all the others.

What decision did you make in childhood that is affecting you now?

Is there a second decision that you are also aware of?

The next step is to counteract each decision with an affirmation. One type of affirmation begins with the words, "I am," and is followed by a positive, desired statement of being. This type of affirmation is effective at counteracting decisions made in early childhood. Sometimes the positive statement seems "a bridge too far;" that is, you can't say it because it is too far removed from who you are and where you are in life right now. It goes against the decision you unconsciously made years ago. It's too good for you and you would feel you were lying. There would be a lot of internal resistance. The Gremlin or Loch Ness monster or who you have in your head would have a lot to say. So if you'd like to say you deserve good things in your life, or you are brave, or worthy, but you really don't feel that way about yourself, one way to get around this resistance is to say that you are *willing to begin to believe* that you deserve good things. No one, not even your internal critic can fault you for being *willing* to do these things or *willing* to want them for yourself. So it's best, if you sense any internal resistance at all, to start your affirmations with the words, "I am willing to begin to believe that I am... "

A young woman, a dental hygienist, had decided that she was "dirty" because of early experiences in her life. That decision led to the statement, "Therefore, I don't deserve good things." This decision prevented her from accepting the good things that did come into her life, including nice young men. The more solidly entrenched a personal decision, the more it affects everyday life and the more difficult it is to eradicate. These decisions, or belief systems, have a lot of power over the individual and are very resistant to change. So an affirmation that stated, "I deserve good things in life," would meet with a lot of internal resistance. An affirmation that began with the words, "I am willing to begin to believe I deserve good things in life," would meet with less resistance. After all, who could argue with the fact that she was *willing to begin to believe* that she could be different?

Another young woman in medical school was having difficulties with negative emotions. She had an old childhood belief that she was not important to others. When situations occurred that reminded her of this belief, her emotions would plummet and she would become tearful and depressed. We went to work on countering this old belief with an affirmation that stated, "I am important." However, she didn't really feel important, and the affirmation felt like a lie to her. It was a "bridge too far." So we added the words, "I'm willing to begin to believe," to her affirmation, "I am important." She found she could comfortably say this to herself without resistance. She repeated the affirmation many times a day. She wrote it down; she said it out loud; she recorded it on a tape and played it in her car.

Eventually she was able to drop the words, "I'm willing," and "I'm beginning to believe." Then she changed the affirmation to read, "I am important to myself and to others." When last seen she was well on her way to counteracting an old, demoralizing belief about herself. She was well on her way to feeling important to herself and to others.

Other belief statements based on childhood decisions that I've discovered during the course of treatment include: "I'll never amount to anything."

"I'm not loveable." "I don't deserve good things in life." "I don't deserve to be thin." "I never do anything right." "I never do anything good enough." "I have to earn it."

Affirmations undo subconscious childhood and adolescent decisions. They can be used to change or eradicate debilitating beliefs that have hung on since childhood.

This type of affirmation can also be used to build and improve positive personal qualities. I used this method when I was preparing to leave the job I'd found upon arriving in Arizona and was getting ready to start my private practice - The Lighthouse Center. I was scared of losing my newly found security. I was immobilized with fears regarding the unknown ahead of me. I was terrified of failure. I wanted to be brave; I needed to be brave; but I wasn't feeling very brave at all. When I tried saying the affirmation, "I am brave," I was met with a lot of resistance and disbelief. So I began my affirmation with the words, "I am willing to begin to believe I am brave." I repeated this affirmation morning, noon and night. When I was driving my car, taking a walk, or in the shower, I repeated these words and other affirming statements. One day I noticed a change. I hadn't started the affirmation with the words, "I am willing…" instead, I'd begin with the words, "I am beginning to feel brave." I continued to repeat this affirmation on a regular basis, and soon the words, "I'm beginning" were gone. I was able to say, "I am brave" without any resistance to the words or any backtalk from the Loch Ness monster.

My level of bravery did improve, and I was able to leave my position and start my private practice as a psychotherapist.

Using affirmations <u>does</u> work. Affirmations are like setting your car on cruise control. Whether you're up or down emotionally, an affirmation can signal to the inside of you how you'd like to be and can help move you toward that desired goal. They can influence your emotions, your thoughts and your actions. Affirmations can move you toward how you want to feel, how you want to think and how you want to act.

Affirmations can be used for very specific purposes. They can be used to address fears, to enhance self-esteem, to build skills, to increase a level of functioning. They can be used to address health problems, smoking cessation and weight reduction.

The following are some examples of affirmations I have used or suggested to others:

I am brave.
I am calm, confident, warm and loving.
I relate with sensitivity.
I am a kind and considerate mom.
I am gentle.
I am dependable.
I communicate with confidence.
I am a person who chooses not to smoke.
I weigh a healthy 126 pounds.
I am focused.
I am balanced.
I simplify my life.
I am filled with joy, light and laughter.
I am healthy, happy and full of energy.
I am worthy of the good things in life.
I can do anything I set my mind to.
I am successful in all aspects of my life.
I build a successful private practice.
I develop a positive professional reputation throughout the valley.
I am open to positive growth and change.
I attract warm and loving people into my life.
I find the perfect position/job.
I am a positive person.

Affirmations are always stated in the present tense, even if the statement is not true yet. To state that "I will" do something always puts it in the future and leaves an undetermined amount of time before the desired behavior change takes place. The present tense statement is more effective in changing behavior.

The uses are many and the options diverse. Write your own to meet your needs and to move you in a direction you desire for yourself. Affirmations, when used daily, keep inner thoughts positive and productive. They help to build qualities you wish to have or wish to increase. They can move you toward improved health. They can heal old beliefs. They give you confidence to remain on a desired path. Say them daily, write them out and post them where you'll see them often. You can put them on a tape or a CD and play it when you're in your car. I've been told that it takes twenty-one days to program yourself with a new belief. My experience has been that long-established negative beliefs are very resistant to change and take much longer to eradicate. Patience, persistence and perseverance are the keys to success. You and your path are worth it!

Take this opportunity to write down three affirmations you could use to make desired changes in your life. Remember to keep them simple, start with "I am…" and if it seems necessary, begin with the words, "I am *willing to begin to believe* I am…"

1.

___

2.

___

3.

___

Whatever keeps you going in the direction of your current goal and your overall purpose is valid. Affirmations work extremely well to counteract doubts that arise. One young woman, who wanted to become a star, was beset by numerous negative messages from many different people. We concentrated on staying focused and not letting doubts get in her way. Affirmations we used to do this included: "The timing is perfect." "My future is assured." "Good comes from expected and unexpected sources." "I am loveable." "I trust the process." "I have faith." "I stay focused."

Perhaps you noticed that she used two different types of affirmations: one set that began with the words, "I am..." and another set of statements that were made up of positive words designed to build trust. The first type of affirmation you have already been working with in order to build desired qualities in yourself. The second type of affirmation I call "affirmations of assurance."

Affirmations of assurance are simple statements of fact that are positive in nature. They are designed to fill your mind with positive thoughts and help ease your doubts and fears. They speak to the Loch Ness monster in your mind, telling it about the abundant support and guidance that is available to you. Some examples of affirmations of assurance are:

My future is assured.
The timing is perfect.
Good things come to me now.
Abundance comes from expected and unexpected sources.
The perfect job is waiting for me.

I also believe that affirmations of assurance draw good things toward you. Remember in Chapter 3 when I said that what you think about expands? I used the example of a trip to Belize and that when I became interested in Belize, then Belize seemed to be everywhere. You attract that which you think about most often. If you want to attract good things into your life, then hold good thoughts in your head. Use affirmations of assurance to attract positive things.

Notice what comes in. If you have asked for money, notice the check that comes in the mail or the loan that is repaid. If you have asked for an answer to a problem, notice the answer that comes from some unexpected source such as a book, a quote, or even a television show. If you have asked for reassurance, pay attention to the song line that repeats and repeats in your brain. If you have asked for love and support notice the friend who calls unexpectedly or the note that arrives in the mail. Often what you've asked for comes in some form *other* than what you expected. Your job – your responsibility – is to notice that it does come in and to give thanks.

These responses to your requests provide assurance that you are on a path. Assurances clean your windows. Assurances wash away the doubts and fears that keep you stuck in one place, that immobilize you, that terrify you so much that you are afraid to take one step forward. On an episode of <u>Northern Exposure</u>, Graham Greene, playing the role of a Native American Shaman said, "Maybe it doesn't matter what road we embark on. What matters is that we embark." Affirmations of assurance help give us the courage to embark on this path of life.

My experience has been that fears and terrors related to change, newness, and unknowns are also very resistant and require serious intervention with affirmations. Take this opportunity to write down three affirmations of assurance that would help you feel more confident on your path.

1.

_____

2.

_____

3.

_____

Personal Notes

Questions:

Thoughts:

Actions:

Chapter 6:

What's Your Scarecrow Doing Now?

What's Your Scarecrow Doing Now?

Sometimes people came to me with complex problems; sometimes they presented simple ones. Usually there would be a sense of feeling stuck or overwhelmed. Often patients lacked insight into where they were with the problem or how it was overwhelming them. One way of getting a handle on the problem was to ask them to visualize a symbol or an image, which would pertain to their problem. There was no trance work involved with this. I didn't use hypnosis. I would just ask them to quiet themselves, close their eyes and go inside their heads to ask one question, "What symbol or symbols would best describe my situation, my dilemma, my problem?" In many cases, my patients would get some sort of picture or symbol.

The idea for this intervention came from the book <u>Personal Power Through Awareness</u> by Sanaya Roman. In her book, the author presented the asking for symbols in the following way:

If there is a situation in your life you would like to resolve, you can always ask for images and symbols that will help you. Think of a situation in your life right now, something you would like an answer to, and ask for a healing image. See if you can get an image of the other person involved, or the entire situation. If you have someone in your life who is causing you trouble, tying up your time and energy, try to see him or her symbolically. He may appear to be coming at you with a battering ram, and you might see yourself as a wall that constantly gives into his force. You could work with the situation by changing and healing the symbols, perhaps imagining the battering ram changing into a tiny piece of cardboard and your wall becoming flexible like rubber. Symbols are, in fact, more direct and more healing than words, for they are not connected to your belief system... It is not necessary to know what they mean to be healed by them.

When working with patients, the meaning of these symbols was not always apparent, but that was all right. At least we had something to work with, something from within the person – like a message from the inside to the outside. Perhaps this message came from the right brain, which thinks in symbols, or perhaps it was a message from the subconscious. Whatever the source of the information, the value of the information was incredible, as we now had something concrete to work with and a means for measuring changes.

A young woman in a secure established relationship found herself becoming restless and withdrawn. She talked about valuing the relationship and then she talked about her desire for activities, schooling, growth and freedom. When asked to picture a symbol that described her situation, she appeared surprised and startled when she got a screen door. And along with the door came a phrase from a song that mentioned wanting "a piece of the sky." We talked about the screen door and whether she was on the inside looking out or on the outside looking in. Of course, with her situation, she was on the inside looking out – and outside was a piece of the sky, her symbol for freedom. When she left the relationship and had the freedom she desired, she discovered that the screen door was still in place. It was more mobile and could swing open with ease. She could step out, but she was not willing to let people in. So, she still doesn't have her freedom. Now her lack of freedom is internal, not external. No longer is someone else keeping

—Who's Walking Around in Your Head with Muddy Boots?—

her from being free. She and her own fears are keeping her from freely expressing herself. The work she has ahead of her is to develop a better opinion of herself, to improve her self-esteem, and not worry so much about what other people think. This is called becoming "inner directed" as opposed to being "outer directed." Then, perhaps, the screen door can be open. It will be a good symbol for measuring progress.

In another case, we used the symbol to measure progress. Deanna had come to me because she always became dysfunctional in relationships. She would flex and bend, trying desperately to become what the other person wanted. When she came to see me, she was looking to satisfy her need for independence and autonomy; she wanted to evolve as a whole person and be able to stay that way in a relationship. Her goal was to become a gold statue, like those given out at the Oscar Award Ceremony. Actually she was using a description of gold that she had found in James A. Michener's novel, Alaska. Gold, as described by Michener, can stand by itself, it doesn't deform when it comes into contact with other elements and it has great persistence. These were her desires for herself – to be able to stand by herself, to not deform when she became involved in a relationship and to persist in being what she was. This was her very specific goal. The image she began with, however, on her way to that goal was, "I'm hot JELL-O with one or two ice cubes. Soupy red JELL-O."

Two months later, after a lot of very hard work in therapy and a lot of success, Deanna's JELL-O had developed into the hard ball stage. She said, "It's rubbery and pretty solid." The shape? "Cylindrical with feet." We were moving in the right direction. The color is still red, cherry red, representing, as she says, The Red Badge of Courage.

Next her JELL-O solidified. She said you could cut letters out of it, as seen on the commercials done by Bill Cosby. "I can be any shape that I choose and maintain it." She was feeling very solid, very grounded and much more in control of herself.

Finally, at the close of our work together, Deanna remarked, "Alone I am now gold. It remains to be seen how I will be when a man comes into my life, but I think it will be much better than ever before."

Another lovely lady, caught between attending to her mother and pleasing her husband, saw herself as a spinning wheel or spinning button with a string on either side. Both mother and husband were pulling on these strings and she was spinning in response to whoever pulled the hardest. She didn't feel that she had any say over her life, but she didn't want to hurt anyone's feelings either. So she was caught in a position of powerlessness. "I am the button."

The symbol of the button being pulled in two different directions accurately portrayed her position. Becoming aware of her powerless position was the first step toward change. Seeing her powerlessness was different from feeling it, because it gave her some leverage to do something. In other areas of her world she was a powerful and effective person. She could now begin to limit the pulling of the strings. She could begin to take charge of her life.

As we worked together, discussing values and priorities, she began to understand how and why she had given her power away. We talked about ways she could begin to reclaim her power. As she grew and changed, her sense of self increased. Her button, or spinning wheel disappeared. In place of the powerless image she had a cute little tractor. One of those that could turn on a dime and do many different things. (I think it's called a Bobcat.) This was a good representational image for her because she was now more mobile, more powerful and capable of doing many things. She had come a long way from the powerless spinning button! However, she did point out that the Bobcat was in limited territory and still on a tether. So there continued to be outer controls in her life that she was well aware of.

Another young woman was caught in a decision dilemma. She had left her husband and didn't know whether to stay away or return to him. She vacillated back and forth, afraid to move in either direction. The day she first came to see me, she described herself as "swimming in the sea all by myself and about to go under." She was emotionally overwhelmed, ready to give up and she wasn't sure she could continue living. We met several times that week to stabilize her emotions and to look realistically at her choices. Naturally, her image changed in response to this support. "Now I'm on a raft. It's a good size. There are small oars and the water is calm and smooth. I can't see the shore. I'm just rowing and at times I'm just sitting. I'm not sure what direction I'm going." At least she no longer felt she was going under. Therapy provided the support of a life raft and the oars represented tools she could use when she had a better idea what direction she wanted to head.

Several weeks later her husband called a meeting to discuss their future. This pressure caused an increase in her anxiety and returned her to the powerless feelings that had brought her to my office in the first place. Her image changed to reflect the insecurity. "I feel like I'm off the raft and a little ways away from it. The good thing is I feel I can get back to it." She did get back to the raft and the oars grew in length as she grew in power. Eventually she reached shore. Her final decision isn't important. What is important is that her symbols and images reflected her situation and they changed as she changed.

Another young woman, when asked to imagine what was getting in the way of progress toward personal growth, discovered that she had a dam inside her. The dam, when asked what it was there for, said that it was for protection, for keeping feelings in and for keeping people out. We talked to the dam and thanked it for protecting her when nothing else was available. We also talked to it about transforming itself into something different that would allow her to experience more positive feelings and facilitate her growth.

When questioned about being transformed, the dam communicated that it was afraid to have nothing there to protect the woman and so agreed to become a screen with wide mesh that the water could come through. Immediately, the woman noticed that leaning up against the new filter was a boulder. This boulder wanted to become a large, bright yellow daisy, but couldn't as long as it represented guilt and debt. The guilt was about not measuring up to her own standards and the debt was about not being all that she could be. We talked about what could happen next. The young woman decided that she needed to forgive herself and get moving with her life. In order to accomplish this, she needed to push the boulder out of the flow of her life. She imagined herself pushing it up a hill and noticed that as she did so, the boulder started growing smaller and smaller.

At the end of this session, this woman had a symbol to work with – the boulder, and she had very specific emotions to work on and resolve – the guilt and the sense of indebtedness. She left feeling empowered by her own images and clear and purposeful about what she needed to do. The answers had come from inside her, from her own imaging. They were messages from herself, to herself and they helped her identify her situation and gave her a standard by which to measure her progress.

I measured my own progress with the help of a jigsaw puzzle. When I envisioned my life in Michigan, the pieces of the jigsaw puzzle fit tightly together. There was no room for growth. Once I moved to Arizona, the puzzle pieces separated leaving space in between them, thus reflecting the new opportunities for personal growth. It was interesting to watch the transformation of the puzzle as I built a life for myself in this new setting. First the space between the puzzle pieces was empty, then a fine mesh appeared, and finally the space was filled with an opaque substance. I still cannot see the final picture, but the puzzle is a whole entity, much larger than the one that existed in Michigan.

I used this puzzle image as an example with a young woman who had been adopted at birth. She did not know much about her heritage and had been told that a search for her birth mother would break her adoptive mother's heart. So we talked about her being like a puzzle. It was interesting that she expressed concern about just what we were going to put in the center of the puzzle. Apparently, in her image, the center was an empty hole.

One week later she returned and announced that there was a mosaic at the center of her puzzle. It was filled with precious gems: rubies and emeralds and topaz, carefully secured with grout. Every time she thought about this mosaic she felt at peace. This image helped her regain her emotional balance and sense of inner security, something she had never had. I worked with her toward achieving a sense of worth and value. Eventually she was able to say that light could shine through the mosaic and in that way she could finally be a person who had value.

Another young woman discovered something of value in her images, her own self-confidence. She was floundering in her profession due to a number of circumstances and had lost confidence in her talents and abilities. She came to see me because she was afraid to take a position that had just been offered to her. It was a wonderful position that would use all her talents and abilities, plus provide her with an opportunity to grow. She wanted to understand what was getting in her way and what was preventing her from moving forward.

When asked to close her eyes and describe the problem in terms of symbols, she said that she was standing in green grass at the edge of a swiftly flowing river. In fact, she said the river was flowing so fast that it scared her. About ten yards from the bank where she was standing, there was a square granite rock in the river that she wanted to get to, but couldn't. As she was agonizing about how to get to that rock, her father appeared rowing a boat. He came over to the shore and took her on board. Then he rowed downstream to a large, quiet lake. They sat in the boat and talked about what had happened to her. She told him about losing her confidence. When asked what her confidence looked like, she described a crystal ball, which materialized in her hands. Her father then offered to provide a special pouch so she would never lose her confidence again. This pouch, she tied to her waist.

The river signified life for her and it was flowing by too fast and too powerfully. She was frightened and felt incapable of negotiating it. She used the words stable and pedestal to describe the square rock. Quite obviously the square stone represented stability. It also represented her desire to be respected for who she was and what she had accomplished. This respect was missing in her life and she did not know how to achieve it. Further questioning revealed that, as the youngest of four children, she had never been respected for her accomplishments. In fact, she had long carried the feeling that she wasn't good enough.

When her confidence emerged as a crystal ball, it had great significance for her. She saw it as something precious, something of value, something that had its own power. She also understood that she had allowed this precious gift to get away from her, that she had lost it. She knew that this confidence was hers and that it was important for her to claim it as her own and to protect it from future loss. Her father's presence helped her bridge the distance between her fears and what she desired for herself. His words validated her and her accomplishments. As the primary family member and the most significant family member in her life, his love and support began to undo the feelings of not being good enough.

When she left the session, she had a better understanding of how her fears and beliefs had been getting in her way. She also understood that she could accomplish much more by claiming her own confidence and building her sense of self-worth. It was much more likely after our work together that she would take the job that has been offered to her and build on that opportunity.

Do you remember a particular wall from Chapter 2? It was described as "Stained glass windows, all different colors, particularly rose, lavender, and brown with a sort of fog at my feet. Sometimes I can see out, sometimes I can't depend what color I'm behind. There's a window that's closed, but not locked. I'm standing on something that is not very supportive, like a wobbly floor."

This is Sarah's wall. Sarah, as you remember, was a young woman trained in the legal profession and suffering from chronic fatigue syndrome. Her life had come to a halt with the fatigue and the depression that are common symptoms of chronic fatigue syndrome. She suddenly had a lot of time on her hands to explore who she was and what she really wanted to do with her life. But she had little energy to implement these thoughts and, with the depression, little hope or enthusiasm that she could act on them. As a result of her illness, her depression and her low energy level, Sarah's wall and images changed slowly and in incremental ways. In four months, Sarah's images had changed to "I'm standing on adobe bricks that are more solid. I can see part of them now. The windows open out and I can see a bird's nest with three new eggs." Sarah felt, and I agreed, that the nest meant she had been successful in finding a home for herself, a place where she would be allowed to incubate in safety with no demands placed on her – a place where she could recuperate and grow. She felt the three eggs represented three aspects of her life that were going to open up. One would probably represent home and family, the other her career and she didn't know what the third egg represented.

Another four months passed and the stained glass window was described with the three eggs in full view. Sarah now feels that the eggs represent who she is as a person, who she is as she relates to the world and her career. Her footing has changed, too. The misty fog around her feet is fading. Sarah is standing on stone bricks and adobe bricks. The stone bricks are under her right foot and the adobe bricks are under her left foot. I think of the phrase, "etched in stone," which means unchangeable. I think of adobe bricks as being more creative, more innovative. Although what we are standing on represents the nurturing and support in our life, an alternate meaning here might have to do with whether or not to use creativity in her life work. She talked about wanting to write, take photographs and act but had never allowed herself the privilege of exploring these avenues. The differences in footing could stand for the different choices regarding those activities or they could stand for active versus passive stances in life. In this case, the right foot would indicate a masculine, take charge attitude toward life, and the left foot would refer to the receptive, feminine mode. There are lots of possibilities here, not one of them is absolute and we don't have to know. Inside Sarah, the meaning is clear. Right foot and left foot have meaning, stone and adobe bricks have meaning and the eggs have meaning. The images will evolve and change as Sarah evolves and changes, the meaning will become clearer as she is ready to receive and understand the message.

A year later, when I called and checked in with her, I found that her images had not changed much in content, only in detail. Sarah was still under the hardship imposed by her illness and her progress was slowed by its impact. Sarah's wall continues to change slowly and to signal her about where she is with herself and her life. Her flooring, her foot placement, her eggs and her vista were all reflections of her inner self. It's important to remember that symbols are more direct than words because they are not connected to our belief system. Remember, "It is not necessary to know what they mean to be healed by them" (Sanaya Roman in <u>Personal Power Through Awareness</u>.)

Anne was another person I asked to visualize a symbol to represent her problem. Her response began a long series of visual images that reflected her problems and her movement toward growth. "When asked to visualize myself as a symbol, the picture of a scarecrow popped into my mind immediately. I thought that was quite funny." She described the scarecrow as stuck on the pole and unable to defend itself from the crows that were pecking at its stuffing. This described her position in her family. She was vulnerable to comments and criticism with no protection and no way to defend herself. She was the scarecrow and the crows were her family members.

A second interpretation of Anne's image could be related to her cancer surgery. She had had a mastectomy and it's possible that the crows pecking at the immobilized scarecrow were symbols of the doctors taking things from her body. Perhaps they also related to the poking, the prodding, and the powerlessness of being the patient. A third interpretation involves negative thoughts. What if the crow's third interpretation involves negative thoughts? What if the crows were negative thoughts that pecked at her and that she felt she was powerless to stop? All of these interpretations could be appropriate.

As we have noticed, images and symbols do not stay constant. Part of us is looking for solutions and resolutions to the disharmony within us. If we are seeking answers and looking for personal growth, we are going to find it. Our images are going to reflect this change. Anne's image changed in this way.

"The scarecrow is still immobile and the crows are still there picking away, but circling high in the sky is an eagle. He's so high I can hardly see him, but I hear his call. The scarecrow doesn't know why hearing the call of the eagle makes it feel hopeful, but it does."

One week later more action was taking place. "The eagle is visible now. He's making swoops past the scarecrow. The crows still want the scarecrow's stuffing but they're not as confident. Actually they're very nervous. They land, hover and try again but the eagle presents a threat to them and they haven't succeeded in getting any stuffing. The scarecrow is still immobile and doesn't like it, but feels safer now."

Emotionally Anne felt very good about the eagle. She didn't know why, she just did. I remember her telling me that she felt relieved just hearing it call. There was a sense that someone or something was coming to her aid.

As symbols and images do, Anne's continued to change as we worked together. These changing symbols were a reflection of this work and her gains; they were symbolic of her own internal improvement and increasing sense of hopefulness. They indicated movement toward growth and personal power. They depicted an improved state of mind.

"The crows are still determined, but the eagle has landed, perched on the limb of a tree in view of the scarecrow and now the scarecrow has some movement in his arms. He's able to keep the crows off. They're still there, but *he's* moving his arms, protecting himself in a limited capacity. He's found some powers he didn't realize he had. And the eagle just sits on the limb, watching, as if to say, "I'm here, I'm strength, I'm powerful and I can crush those crows with my talons in a moment, but I want you to rid yourself of their destructive behavior so *you* try and I'll be here to watch over you 'til you're free."

The eagle could be related to many things. It could symbolize God, it could be her subconscious power, it could be her Higher Self. It can stand for whatever is useful for her to believe or for her to know. Someone on the outside can only guess at the possible meanings and implications of the symbols. The person on the inside, the person whose symbol it is, can have a strong sense of the symbol. The symbol may encompass many meanings. Anne's eagle seems to represent power, safety, rescue, or a threat to others who are endangering her. It is someone who is in her favor.

If we look at the possible meanings and interpretations of her "scarecrow" and relate them to the various meanings for the eagle, the eagle may symbolize her need to claim her own personal power and take charge of the crows that are her family members. The eagle may symbolize God being there for her and defending her from the disease and the medical professionals who treat it. If we describe the crows as her own negative thoughts, the eagle may represent her need to take charge of her thoughts and improve her mental attitude. The eagle can mean any and all of these. There may be others not mentioned here. Whatever one can find to make sense of a symbol is helpful, but understand that the subconscious already knows the meaning of the symbol. The meaning is captured in the symbol and is encapsulated in the image. Words may limit the meaning or reduce the meaning. Anne's eagle may have many meanings or it may have one meaning that applies to all the cases. We don't need to know. At some level, she knows.

Anne's story continues: "The scarecrow is starting to pull away from the pole. At first he finds he can lift his arms. He starts to reach up and knock off the crows. The crows try another tactic. They go around and attack from the back. What they don't realize and until this moment, the scarecrow wasn't aware of either, is that his spine has started to separate from the pole. He is not dependent on it for support. He's getting his very own backbone now. And he's angry. He's fighting back. He's not willing to just hang on the pole and accept unacceptable behavior. Enough is enough! He may not be able to stand completely on his own two feet yet, but he is getting stronger each day and with each attack of the crows."

"But the eagle, I don't know where he is. The scarecrow wasn't aware the eagle was not present while he was battling the crows and now that he has temporarily warded them off, he looks for the eagle and the eagle is no where to be found. Scarecrow continues to look. He searches the sky and the fields, he listens for the sounds of him… but cannot hear him… cannot see him."

The eagle went out of sight when Anne began to change and grow stronger, when she could defend herself. The eagle departed when she developed a backbone and could stand on her own two feet. It is possible that all of the strength and power that the eagle stood for on the outside became part of her on the inside. When she had internalized these qualities, the eagle disappeared. The eagle had served its purpose and no longer needed to be in sight. My sense is that the eagle is nearby, ready to return should she need its strength or its protection.

Anne's story goes on as she continues to experience life and to grow and to change. But for you, the reader, her story ends here and yours begins.

Workbook Page

What about you? What problem of yours would you like to have more understanding about? What problem of yours could use some insight? Let's see what we can find out for you.

Find a comfortable position in a place where you can sit quietly and not be disturbed. As you breathe gently, close your eyes and go inside your head. Ask for a symbol or for images that will represent your problem. See what appears. Notice the details. Don't judge or evaluate, just take it all in. If you want, ask for a song or movie title to go with it. Or you can ask for a line from a song or poem that joins with the image. Notice what you get. Notice how you feel about the image and the information contained in any words. You might inquire, of yourself, if the symbol has meaning for you and what that meaning might be. If no answer comes immediately, wait for understanding. Also wait to see what happens to that image. Wait to see how it changes. Watch the changes with interest and curiosity. They can be very interesting!

What symbol did you get?

_____

_____

_____

What was around it or on it that you noticed?

_____

_____

_____

Did you notice anything else?

_____
_____
_____

Did it change in any way as you were watching it?

_____
_____
_____

What information did the symbol provide regarding the question you asked?

_____
_____
_____

What do you know now that you didn't know before?

_____
_____
_____

Personal Notes

Questions:

Thoughts:

Actions:

Chapter 7:
What Does Your Path Look Like?

What Does Your Path Look Like?

This chapter begins with a question similar to the query about animal preferences and the description of your wall. Simply, what does your path look like? What color is it? What is it made of? Is it rough and rocky or smooth and easy? Is it visible or hard to distinguish? Have many people walked this path before or just a few? What does the landscape and terrain look like? What kind of foliage is around it? What time of day is it? What is the weather like? Are you standing still or moving? How is your energy level? If you look behind you, what do you see? If you look ahead, what do you see? Are there obstacles or barriers in your pathway? What do they look like? Always ask, is there anything interesting or different about your path?

Take a few moments to describe your path, using the questions above for guidelines. Or, take a separate piece of paper and draw your path.

_____

_____

_____

Remember that there are no right or wrong answers to these questions and there is no right or wrong result to this exercise. There is only your own creativity and information to be discovered about yourself. The answers range from very simple to very complex. They differ from time to time, depending on what is happening in your life or what you focus on. All answers have meaning related to some aspect of your life. Sometimes the answers show you where you are stuck or lend insight into where you are right now.

The simplest path described to me came from a young woman with two children whose husband wanted out of the marriage. Initially, she was terrified of this; she saw herself as powerless and incapable of handling such a drastic change. However, when she addressed her fears and discovered the courage to tackle her problem, her path looked like this:

"It's a white path that is blank ahead. Behind me it's dark." White, as you remember from the chapter on walls, represented the color or purity and the empty page on which life is yet to be written. Ahead was "blank" – empty, a void to be lived since she could not imagine life any different than the past. Behind her was dark – a shade of misery and unhappiness.

Remember, just as there was no right or wrong animal and there was no right or wrong wall, there is no right or wrong path. There is just information from the self to the self, about the place you find yourself in life. The information can be very simple or it may be detailed, as described next.

—Who's Walking Around in Your Head with Muddy Boots?—

A young man named Mike had a tan dirt path with curves. There was tall crab grass on either side that needed to be mowed. It hadn't been tended to. Somebody else had made the path and it had been heavily traveled. Behind was black and ahead there was no end to the path. "It goes to the horizon," Mike said.

Mike's background included severe childhood neglect and abuse. In response to emotional deprivation, he became a hellion who didn't care what happened to him. Consequently, when he looked back at his past, all was black. Black represented a loud "No" to the situation he found himself in and his anti-social behavior was a response to that "No." The path he traveled on had obviously been traveled by many rebellious teens before him. He was never tended to, never had attention, and this was represented in the grass that needed mowing. It seems possible that "needing mowing" also refers to the need for discipline. In his case, Mike is beginning to provide the self-discipline. Crabgrass could refer to his tendency to be irritable or it could refer to being a "weed" in society. Mike's future appears to be more positive and long lasting than his past. Much of this is due to his positive outlook and the changes he is making in his life.

Another young man described his path as big and open with little trails that branched off it. He said that every once in a while he would return to the major pathway. As you might imagine, this man is a teen-ager and the path very aptly describes his current activities. He has indeed gotten in trouble several times, but has not become lost. Each time he has managed to return to the behavior that is expected and required by his family.

Another path description that involved getting lost concerned a man named Joel. He had been in trouble with the law, had learned many lessons regarding his behavior, and was well aware of the temptations that confronted him. He described his path as "focusing straight ahead toward the bright light, almost like being on a conveyor belt." He did not want to take the off-ramp to the "gray and dusty sides of the road." The sides of his path were littered with beer bottles, marijuana, hookers, depression and bad business dealings. It was like a big dust storm where one could lose his way. He could choose to go off the path, but if he did "screw up," he would lose that day forever. And if he went more than ten feet off the path he might get lost and not be able to find his way back. Of great importance to him was the awareness that he always had a choice about where he could walk on this path.

"My path is rocky and narrow and very steep. There are big pine trees on either side with vines and moss at my feet. Even though it's mid-day, it's dark out. When I look back, there is a cliff behind me and when I look ahead, it's steep. I'm tired and don't know if I can get up the path. It just feels like death. Strangely enough, I hear an owl further on." This was the path of a man whose wife had left him the year before. His existence changed with her departure as he assumed responsibility for raising their three children. The cliff represented the end of the marriage and the rocky path represented the difficulties he had experienced ever since. His clinging to old ways and established beliefs about marriage and family were symbolized by the moss and vines at his feet. When he couldn't change events he became seriously depressed, evidenced by the darkness and his tiredness. He became so depressed that some thoughts of suicide came through, as well. Up ahead there was an owl. Owls represent two things to me – wisdom and death. In many cultures, owls symbolize wisdom. In the book, <u>I Heard the Owl Call My Name</u>, Margaret Craven wrote a story that included the beliefs of the Kwakiutl Indians of British Columbia. One of their beliefs is that the owl calls the name of the man who is going to die. I'd like to think that this gentleman would become wiser and more mature in dealing with changes in his life. If there is a death, then I would like it to be the death of the old ways and old beliefs that are currently holding him back. There is always the possibility that the owl represents his own actual death. I hope that our work together will provide him with opportunities other than that sort of death. I hope our work will make it possible for him to have a positive future.

I worked closely with the small business development center of a local college. I trained and counseled female entrepreneurs there. At a workshop one young entrepreneur described a lush path with abundant foliage along side of her and ahead of her. The path was clearly marked and easy to travel. Unfortunately, she was stuck. Her feet just would not move. They wouldn't lift up and her toes wouldn't wiggle.

We talked about the plans for her business venture and the steps she would need to take for the venture to be a reality. Then we talked about the fears immobilizing her. She was afraid to step forward into the venture. I had her visualize herself on this path, and we worked on her feet until she could move just one toe. Toes, according to Louise Hay's book, <u>You Can Heal Your Life</u>, represent the details in life. Feet represent your ability to be self-supporting, as to "stand on our own two feet," your ability to be mobile or to take steps forward. So, if this young woman could begin to attend to the details of her business venture, she would soon be able to move her foot and eventually, both feet. Then, she would be able to move ahead with her plans. She was amazed that visualization could reveal so much. The result was that she was pleased at the insight gained and hopeful that she would no longer be stuck.

When you are aware of where you are, then you can make changes. Until you know, you operate from a position of blindness. You can't change that which you don't know. The young woman whose feet were stuck on the path had a sense that she was not moving ahead but she didn't fully realize it until she saw it for herself. She couldn't change the immobilization until she knew it existed. Once she knew, it was something she could work on. Perhaps, if she could cause a toe to move, she could then consciously free up more and more of her feet, until she became mobile.

Another struggling entrepreneur visualized her path as "very straight, a soft dirt road with ruts. The surrounding terrain is desert with mountains ahead. Actually there are two layers of mountains, the smaller foothills, then rounded big ones. It's 10 a.m. and the weather is warm and clear."

In this case, one of the key words was "ruts." This woman was in a rut when it came to availing herself of new business opportunities. She responded out of old patterns and produced "arid" results. Ahead, all she saw were more difficulties and struggles, as symbolized by mountains. She was not happy with her path but grateful for the insight it gave her.

I ran into this woman six months later at a workshop I was presenting. I learned that her path had changed considerably. She proudly told me that her path was no longer rutted and the arid desert was replaced by a lake and rich vegetation. Also, the mountains had disappeared, replaced by a rich, appealing landscape. Not only had her path changed but her business world had changed, as well. Business was flourishing and she was looking ahead to even better days financially. She commented to the class that knowing about her path was the finest tool she'd ever been taught.

Using visualization is a way of working on the inside from the outside. Using visualization is a way of letting the outside know what is happening on the inside. Using visualization is a way of measuring progress and improvement as in the last case. There, the desert and rutted path were reflecting entrepreneurial disaster or more failure. With that information, and awareness that changes could be made, this young businesswoman took charge of her life, significantly changed her thinking and revised her actions. The new and improved path signifies abundance and a positive future ahead. It reflects the improvements she's made. This entrepreneur can use her path as a barometer to constantly let her know how she's doing and how she is viewing her current situation.

A woman, who had been a schoolteacher and had always valued security and structure, saw herself in a long corridor. There were many doors along this corridor, but none of them were open. She did notice, however, that at the far end, the corridor turned. For some reason she began organizing her desk and cleaning out her files in preparation for a change in jobs. That change came within three months, and suddenly she was around the corner of her corridor holding a position that enabled her to fly from place to place and teach other teachers. She was also part of the publishing world, an arena she had always wanted to explore. She then held a position with much less structure and more freedom than she has ever held previously.

Two years later, she is self-employed and working all over the country on a contractual basis. Her path is outside now. It opens up on a veranda that is up high. There is a beautiful view that is light and bright. The expanse is magnificent. It is early morning. She has more energy, both physical and emotional. And she has the sense that something wonderful is going to happen. She has moved from structure and security to openness and options. She has new goals and feels limitless. In fact her experience reminds me of a motivational quote by Walpole, "Men are often capable of greater things than they perform. They are sent into the world with bills of credit, and seldom draw to their full extent." She is drawing on her bill of credit and using it to her full advantage.

I had a path in my mind before I moved from Michigan to Arizona. First, there was a bridge and then a wide sandy hiking path traveled heavily by others. Then there appeared a much smaller path that left the main road and scrambled up to the right. It showed little sign of travel and was distinctly a more physically challenging path than the other. This smaller path was my path. I left a thriving practice in Michigan and drove clear across the country to the state of Arizona where I knew only two people. Challenging indeed!

A more recent path has emerged as I write this book and attempt to contact publishers for approval. This path actually begins under the roof of a porch. It's dark and shaded under there. Just ahead is a sidewalk, which turns to the right because there is a wall directly ahead with vines climbing all over it. The sidewalk directly ahead is in the shade too, but if I keep walking along it, and now, to the right, it comes out into the sunshine and a broad open meadow with wild flowers, people, laughter and happiness.

The roof represents a mental lid that is present as I write this book. I've never authored a book before, so there is some part of me that says, "I can't do this." Like the people with ceilings and domes over their walls, someplace inside me doesn't believe I can write a book or have it published. The dimness and shade represent doubts. Who will read this book? Who will want to publish it? What if it isn't good enough to publish? Ahead is a wall, a barrier with vines. Vines represent old beliefs and old ways of a publisher who may not be accustomed to a book of this nature! Notice, if I continue to the right (write) I will come out into the sunshine and abundance. That's the part of my visualization that is keeping me going. I'm not going to stay in the shade; I'm headed toward the sunshine.

More about paths – Spiritual Paths

While hiking with friends on Squaw Peak in Phoenix, Arizona, one 14 year old expressed anxiety over where we were, even though her parents, who were with us, had hiked there numerous times. She kept asking if we were lost. Her mother and father kept reassuring her that we would not get lost and that we would get to where we were going. Nothing expressed by either parent seemed to allay the girl's anxiety.

I think we are like that on our path through this life. We can't "see" where we are going. We don't realize there are roads and trails and maps and we are all going to get where we're going. Like this teenager, we are worried about every step of the way. We doubt, we fear, we need reassurance. The path is clearly there but we just don't trust it. We don't trust what I call the Universe. All paths lead to Rome, as the saying goes. Our path leads home. There is nowhere else to go. There is no place else that we can end up. Our path will bring us home. We determine what we will accomplish along the way. It's up to us what we do with ourselves on this trip. It is up to us to individually determine our pace. It's up to each of us to learn lessons and to grow.

In some ways there is a path already laid out for us. It began when we came into the world or maybe before that. Like a tree, its size and shape are determined before it grows. An oak tree is determined in the acorn. A rose's color, size and shape are determined before the bud is formed. An animal's size and shape, like that of a cat, are determined in the embryo. Who we are and what we are to become is all there on the inside, waiting to evolve, waiting for us to wake up to it.

A mature gentle man, named Tony, knew he was supposed to be learning a lesson; he just wasn't sure what that lesson was. Having the sense that he was on a path helped him feel the purpose of the happenings in his life. These events weren't random. He wasn't the victim of random, purposeless events. His path was rocky and dusty, with cacti on either side. It went uphill and he couldn't see where it was going. "It will be a difficult hill, but I have the energy it requires." He continued to want to know where he was going. I often stressed the need to value the trip and not focus on the destination. As he proceeded on his journey toward healing an old wound, he discovered that his path changed, it was smoothing out. This visual change greatly reinforced his internal growth and personal development. We decided during a recent session, that his journey might not be toward a "doing" goal, but instead might be a "being" goal. I recalled and quoted Wayne Dyer's comment, from <u>You'll See It When You Believe It,</u> "We are not human doings, we are human beings." This made great sense to Tony.

Paths are not something you can compare. Actually how you are doing on your path is not open for comparison. "Comparisons," according to my grandmother's saying, "are odious," meaning it's not good to compare. We get unexplained bad feelings when we do.

When we look to see how another person is doing on their path, we automatically compare ourselves to them and usually not favorably. We are human and we do this. We look to see if someone is farther ahead and we compare ourselves. Maybe they are going faster, making more money or seem to have more success. What we compare ourselves to is a reflection of the values that are important to us. If we are a teenager, we compare ourselves to someone else's looks or job or grades or automobile. Young women often compare size, shape, hair color, weight and the looks of the gentlemen they are dating. Men compare and compete about their job, athletic ability, car, who they are dating, bank account, size of house, etc. Even in the world of self-growth and spiritual growth there are comparisons. Who is growing faster, who is more spiritual, who is manifesting more of what they want?

It's best just to keep our eyes on the path ahead and to look within rather than without. Everyone is on his or her own path and we cannot know what another's path is all about. We cannot know what lesson they came here to learn. We cannot judge what challenges they set out for themselves. One person may choose to climb Squaw Peak, another, the Grand Canyon, a third Mount Everest. Is one any better than the other? Is one any less than the other? Each one is an individual challenge. All are worthy paths.

Another way is to think of it is in terms of math and school. Is the child in kindergarten learning about numbers any less important than the third grader who is learning about multiplication? And is the math learned by a third grader any less important than the algebra learned by a high school student? Is the college student learning calculus superior to the high school student? Is one student any better or any worse than the others? No. They are all learning. They are just at different stages.

On the other side of that coin, the student who knows calculus need not feel awkward or ashamed of his knowledge and experience. He is not presenting himself as being superior to the student who is just learning to add and subtract. He happens to have progressed beyond that point. He has learned more lessons. There is no shame in knowing calculus. Nor is there shame in being spiritually awake.

And so you are on a path, a spiritual path. Bernie Siegle, MD, regularly asks his patients for a "path report." He's very aware of paths and he wants his patients to be aware of them, too. His question is, "How are you doing on your path?" Let's say that this spiritual path is different from the growth path immediately in front of you. Let's say that this spiritual path has a description all its own. So take a moment now to get quiet, close your eyes and ask for an image to describe your spiritual path. Notice what comes in. Look it over. See it, sense it, smell it, hear it. Write it down or draw it. Use the space provided or your own paper or a journal you are keeping.

Describe your spiritual path:

_____

_____

_____

Now look at your answers closely and ask:

How is my spiritual path different from my current or growth path?
___
___
___

What meaning does this have for me?
___
___
___

What do I know now about where I am on my path?
___
___
___

What assurances are built into my path?
___
___
___

What can I take away that will assist me or reassure me?
___
___
___

Jackie's current path is a dirt footpath. It's overgrown with greenery and winds its way ahead. Sun is streaming through the clouds. The time is early afternoon and her energy is "lazy." There's an opening way back behind her, like an entrance. Ahead she sees the path continuing, but there's no exit visible. She feels uncertainty.

By comparison, her spiritual path is much more concrete and positive. She is walking up stairs made of greenish-tan granite. It's a very structured path with well-manicured bushes on either side. Her energy is high and she feels apprehensive, but confident. Ahead is bright light. Above there's blue sky. And there's soothing, spiritual music playing in the air.

Karen's life path is brown dirt, not muddy and not rocky, just brown dirt. It wanders back and forth, and heads up a hill. She can't see over the hill so she doesn't know what's on the other side. Along the path are trees, old trees that have grown up in an old neighborhood where they have grown so big that they have to be cut away to allow passage underneath. These trees get less dense further along the path.

When asked what her spiritual path looked like, Karen saw the same path as above, but instead of dirt there was water flowing up hill and she was riding on some sort of surfboard! What does that tell you about the ease of a path? About the sureness of being on a path? About how you can't get lost?

Affirmations on Your Path

Karen needed to believe that her path really existed. She needed to have confidence in her path because major decisions about moving rested on her, so she used positive affirmations to keep her going: "The time is right for this journey." "When I go up there, doors are going to open." "I know I'm going to find the perfect thing to do." She discovered that the road to her new home was the tree-lined road that she had observed in her original path description. "Those are the trees I saw. I know I'm on the right path." Confidence was established.

While striving to maintain confidence on the path brought me to Arizona, I used the affirmation, "The Universe did not bring me all the way out here to fail." While waiting for my practice to build, while wondering where my first patients were going to come from, I kept affirming that I was in the right place at the right time, and the Universe was not going to waste this resource (me). I used the phrase, "Your cup must be empty before it can be filled," to explain the time without seeing patients.

As I write this now my spiritual path looks a lot like the cover of the game "Chutes and Ladders," but with a few differences. The chutes are missing but the ladders extend from cloud to cloud. While doubting and questioning the possibility of actually being an author, one of the ladders appears to have a rung missing. It materializes and disappears even as I watch. I guess I have to step up a little higher to attain the next rung. "Effort only fully releases its reward after a person refuses to quit." (Napoleon Hill)

We're all on a current path for lessons and a spiritual path for growth. It's important to remember that our future and our destination are assured. Learning to believe in this path, to understand it and to trust in it, can make our journey though this life more productive, more satisfying and more enjoyable. We don't have to feel so anxious about where we're going. We can say things to ourselves that will help reassure us. We can grow and have new experiences. I think we were meant to do this while we're here. Your path is secure and your destination is assured. Relax and enjoy the trip.

Personal Notes

Questions:

Thoughts:

Actions:

Conclusion

Conclusion

And so we have reached the conclusion of this book. But this isn't really the conclusion. It is actually the beginning. Perhaps it is the beginning of your personal growth work. Perhaps it is the beginning of your going within to discover answers. Maybe it is the beginning of your seeing yourself as a creative person. For some, it is the beginning of using inner tools to understand themselves better, to clarify problems, and to heal. All beginnings are an entry into new territory. Please don't do as some of my clients do, and berate yourself for not doing this sooner. You couldn't; you didn't know about these tools before now. And please be gentle with yourself if you don't do this perfectly or don't understand all the answers you get. I've tried to stress all along that there are no right or wrong answers. There are just the answers that are presented to us when we ask. Sometimes we understand and sometimes we don't. Sometimes the meaning becomes clear later on. Be patient with the answers and with yourself. Give yourself credit for trying something new. Give yourself a pat on the back for experimenting with something you've never tried before. Keep on asking yourself questions, looking for solutions and clarifications and answers. You'll get new answers and with them, new self-understanding.

Sometimes the answers or symbols change. This change is significant because it represents a change in you. I recently had the experience of having a symbol change on me. When I present workshops on stress management, I always include a segment on Life Purpose. It is one of my beliefs that if you have a sense of purpose, then you understand why you are doing what you are doing in your life. If you know about your sense of purpose then you can handle much more stress in your life. So, for workshops on stress management, I include a relaxation experience for the participants and ask for a sign or symbol that represents their purpose in life. Of course, my own mind answers this question as well. For three or four years my purpose has been a series of concentric circles. This symbol looks a lot like a bulls-eye. For me it has symbolized a pebble dropped in a still pond. The pebble dropped in a still pond sends ripples out and out and out. My purpose has been to reach people and make a difference in their lives. When I touch someone's life, I make a difference in his or her life. When I touch someone's life, I make a difference in their life and that difference makes a difference in others' lives as well. The good goes on as it also goes out to others.

That set of concentric circles had been with me since I left Michigan. It changed in the middle of preparation for a workshop. My new symbol presented itself as an umbrella. Now what could an umbrella possibly have to do with one's purpose in life, especially my life? I thought about the symbol and at first had no understanding of it. Then it dawned on me that the umbrella was protective and represented my role in the new family I had created. This symbol wasn't about my work so much as it was about my personal life. I was to be the protector from the elements. With that insight, the symbol made sense and gave me a very nice sensation of contentment and redefined purpose.

Then, just as I had adjusted to the umbrella as an image of my role in this family, it changed again! Suddenly I had a spinnaker instead of an umbrella. For those of you who have never sailed or are unfamiliar with the sailing world, a spinnaker is the huge billowy sail that is set at the front of the boat and pulls the sailboat smoothly downwind (often toward the finish line in a race). Spinnakers are always the most colorful sail on the boat and, I think, the largest. For me, the spinnaker image was an expansion of the umbrella symbol. The spinnaker was shaped like an umbrella; it was curved and held air. But the spinnaker image was a much more powerful image because it was an active participant. It pulled the sailboat ahead rather than just protecting it. I loved it!

This book was written for your growth and your personal development, but you are not the only one who has grown. During the process of writing this book there has been much growth for me as well and many beginnings, too. Entering the world of writing and publishing has been the beginning of doing something different. A motto I used in 1993 and 1994 was, "Unless you try to do something beyond what you have already mastered, you will never grow." (Ralph Waldo Emerson) And writing this book has certainly been beyond my area of mastery! Or, perhaps I should say it has been beyond my field of comfortable mastery. The gathering of information was not that difficult and even though writing is something I'd never done before, I still perceived it as beyond my area of expertise and therefore difficult. So writing a book for the first time was a new beginning.

Writing this book has also been the beginning of my seeing myself as a creative person. When I was growing up, my sister received compliments about her creativity and I received compliments about being smart. Do you know how difficult it is to write a book when you don't view yourself as a creative person? It's almost impossible. My mind kept saying, "You can't be writing a book because you're not creative. Your sister is the creative one." I had to battle this internal belief throughout the entire writing process. As a result I now tell parents to compliment their children about many positive qualities, not just the most obvious ones.

Writing this book has also caused me to use the tools of guided visualization more and more often with clients. It has also prompted me to expand the types of questions I asked. I began asking questions about anger. "What does your anger look like? Where did the anger come from? What precipitated the anger? What needs to happen so that the anger does less damage?" I even asked questions about the damage. "If there was damage done during childhood, or since then, what does it look like? Where is it in your body? What color is it? What is the damage about? Where did it come from or what caused it?" I asked questions about life purpose, such as the ones I talked about earlier in this chapter. I began to explore the containers people had for compliments. One of the things I discovered was that many people were unable to take in compliments and didn't have so much as a post office box in which to receive them, so they sent them away! In order to grow and build self-esteem, I knew it was very important for them to be able to say and think good things about themselves. If they couldn't take in a compliment, then there was no building up of positive self-regard. Having a receptacle or container for compliments was one of the ways to build this very necessary component.

All of these questions and insights about personal growth and healing will soon be a part of my new book, but I want your input, too. I want to know about your successes with the questions in this book. I want to hear about your symbols and what they mean to you. I want to read your stories about how the tools provided in this book helped you to understand yourself better. I want to learn about your creativity and your discoveries. After all, the sub-title of this book states that it provides tools for self-discovery and self-healing. I want to know what you've discovered. It is my hope that you discovered a treasure chest full of resources, answers and solutions. It is my greatest wish that this exploration into yourself brought about greater understanding, healing and peace of mind. Write to me and it's very possible that your discoveries will become part of my next book. My address is:

>Sabra J. House, LCSW
>The Lighthouse Center, Inc.
>10752 N 89th Place, Suite 113
>Scottsdale, AZ 85260

Good luck and I look forward to hearing from you!

Love and Light,

Sabra

Suggested Reading

Bain, Gabriel Hudson. *Living Rainbows, A Book About Auras.*

Bowers, Barbara. *What Color is Your Aura?*

Butler, Pamela. *Talking to Yourself.*

Carson, Richard. *Taming Your Gremlin.*

Covey, Stephen R. *Seven Habits of Highly Effective People.*

Craven, Margaret. *I Heard the Owl Call My Name.*

Dyer, Wayne W. *You'll See It When You Believe It.*

Frankl, Victor E. *Man's Search for Meaning.*

Gawain, Shakti. *Creative Visualization.*

Gawain, Shakti. *Living in the Light.*

Hay, Louise. *You Can Heal Your Life.*

Hay, Louise. *The Power is Within You.*

Hill, Napoleon. *Think and Grow Rich.*

Jeffers, Susan. *Feel the Fear and Do It Anyway.*

John-Roger and Peter McWilliams. *You Can't Afford the Luxury of a Negative Thought.*

Langer, Ellen J. *Mindfulness.*

Luscher, Max. *The Luscher Color Test.*

Mella, Dorothee L. *The Language of Color.*

Robbins, Anthony. *Awaken the Giant Within.*

Robbins, Anthony. *Unlimited Power.*

Roman, Sanaya. *Personal Power Through Awareness.*

Ziglar, Zig. *See You At The Top.*

Sabra

Sabra's private practice, The Lighthouse Center, Inc, is located in Scottsdale, Arizona. The "Lighthouse" portion of her practice's name was chosen as it represents her Michigan roots and incorporates her last name. But mostly, Sabra chose the image of the lighthouse because she knows that her life path is to serve as a beacon of light for others when they are in darkness.

Patti DuBois enjoys illustrating books and is currently working on illustrations for a children's book. She is a Professional Business Coach, as well as an artist, and resides in Phoenix with her two dogs, Cicely and Solomon. To contact Patti, please email her at sculptorgirl@cox.net.

A companion Compact Disk and Journal set for *Who's Walking Around In Your Head With Muddy Boots* is now available!

On the CD, Sabra has recorded seven separate guided meditations – each of which is drawn from a chapter in the book. The journal is provided for you to record your personal impressions after each meditation and will help you track and reflect upon your personal changes.

Please request more information or order by emailing MuddyBootsCD@aol.com. The cost is $18 for the CD and Journal, plus the shipping and handling fee of $3.00. Your CD and Journal will be mailed out to you promptly.

Printed in the United States
50210LVS00004BA/40